WHY CHRISTIANS CRACK UP!

WHY CHRISTIANS CRACK UP!

MARION H. NELSON, M.D.

MOODY PRESS
CHICAGO

PREFACE

THE QUESTION as to why many Christians develop
emotional or mental disorders, loosely referred to as nervousness,
is a subject of much discussion among Christians. Some feel that
there is no valid reason for a Christian to be nervous. They argue
that the benefits of Christianity for this life are sufficient to prevent any such disorder. "Since the Lord can do anything, why
can't He cure a Christian with a nervous problem?" they ask.
Others feel that mental suffering always stems from personal
spiritual failure or sin. All of these attitudes create an aura of
misunderstanding around the problem.

The idea that a Christian can know perfect mental peace at
every moment is unrealistic and unscriptural. The fact is that
Christians can suffer from any medical or psychological disorder
that affects the rest of mankind. Even Christ was not in perfect
mental peace at every moment, as proven by the gospel accounts
of His times of conflict (Matt. 26:37-39; Mark 14:33-34; Luke
22:44; John 12:27).

Nervous Christians receive a lot of advice, some useless and
some that only helps relieve a few symptoms of their disorder.
They are either given sympathy and encouragement or criticism
and exhortation to straighten up and exercise more faith in God.
They are either pampered or rebuked. Friends usually urge
them to read the Bible, pray, and commune with God. All such
measures may give temporary or partial relief of symptoms, but
they fail to cure the disease. To get permanent relief one must
remove the cause of the symptoms.

In this book I have taken up the different causes of nervousness

5

in Christians as a help to lay people as well as pastors, counselors, physicians, and psychiatrists who are faced with such problems either in themselves or in others.

Some terms I have used should be common to anyone who knows the Lord Jesus Christ as his personal Saviour and who is somewhat familiar with the Bible. These terms may be confusing to a psychologist or psychiatrist who is not well acquainted with the Scriptures. For example, when I refer to God or Satan speaking to a person, I do not mean that the Christian hears an audible, spoken voice; this would be abnormal. I rather refer to the fact that both God and Satan may communicate with men by implanting certain thoughts or convictions in their minds. Verses such as Proverbs 16:1, 9; 21:1; Philippians 2:13; and Revelation 17:17 clearly indicate that God exercises a certain amount of control over the minds of men.

Satan is also able to influence our thinking. In Acts 5:4 it is said that Ananias "planned the evil deed in his heart." But in Acts 5:3 Peter asked Ananias, "Why did Satan fill your heart to deceive God?" So Satan had something to do with the evil plan also. Both Ananias and Satan were responsible for the thought.

Such expressions of the communication of God or Satan with man should not be misunderstood by the person who is familiar with Christian terminology. Other terms which are more strictly medical or psychological are explained where necessary.

My sources of reference have been the Bible, general medical knowledge, and the specialized area of psychiatry. I have tried to synthesize the pertinent facts from all of these areas.

The first edition of *Why Christians Crack Up* was written before I became a psychiatrist. It covered only medical and spiritual reasons why Christians become nervous. In this revision, I have included more information, especially in the psychological area, and have also attempted to clarify certain ideas originally presented in the first book.

I want to acknowledge the help of Haddon W. Robinson and Howard G. Hendricks, professors at Dallas Theological Seminary, who reviewed the manuscript and made many helpful suggestions.

My prayer is that all readers, but particularly the saints of God, may find this book useful in developing more of an understanding of themselves and of others who are in emotional distress.

TABLE OF CONTENTS

Chapter One

A UNIFYING CONCEPT

IT IS NECESSARY to begin with a unifying concept in order to establish the proper relationship of physical, psychological, and spiritual disorders. The concept which properly applies is that of God's regulation of the universe by so-called natural laws. In Colossians 1:16 Paul states that all things were created by the agency of God. In 1:17 he continues to explain that it is by the agency of Him that all things consist (literally, are holding together). This principle makes it clear that the universe is being held together by God. The process by which God regulates the universe involves a system of natural laws.

For instance, when one studies chemistry and physics he observes that matter behaves according to definite laws. By learning what these laws are, he can predict the behavior of a certain chemical in a certain reaction. In the area of astronomy it is clear that the stars follow a fixed course precisely on schedule. God's laws regulate this.

In the study of the human body, we discover many laws which regulate the function of the body. Let us call them physical laws. One such law is that a person must eat food and drink water or his body will suffer and not function as it should and will eventually die.

In the area of the mind we see that the condition of the body affects the brain, and thus the mind is subject to the influence of bodily disorders. A diseased body may result in a mind that functions improperly. We also find that there is a set of psychological laws which affect the way the mind works. For in-

11

stance, a person tends to avoid anything painful and frustrating. A stimulus that is painful may automatically produce a withdrawal response in the mind, such as the desire of a student to stay home from school on the day of a difficult exam. Another law is that when a person works too much his mind becomes fatigued. Unless he allows himself sufficient recreation and relaxation, his mind will not continue to function properly.

Spiritual laws also affect our psychological condition as Christians. A good example is Galatians 6:7-8 which warns that a person who lives a life filled with sins of the flesh (that is, sows to the flesh) suffers eventual damage to himself (that is, reaps corruption).

Our adjustment to all these laws affects the way we feel. Thus, when a Christian develops nervousness or symptoms of mental illness, it may stem from a maladjustment in any one or all of these three areas. A physical disease may be either the cause or the effect of psychological stress and feelings of anxiety. Similarly, a psychological problem may result in a spiritual failure, or vice versa.

In order to remedy the condition of maladjustment, one must determine in what category the trouble lies. If it is a physical disease, then medical treatment should be prescribed. If it is a psychological problem, making the Christian nervous and less effective as a person and leading to spiritual failures, then it must be treated as a psychological problem. A spiritual problem that is secondary to a psychological problem requires psychological help as well as spiritual remedies (such as prayer, reading the Bible, exhortation, etc.).

I make no distinction between psychological and emotional problems, as they are identical. A psychological problem exists behind the disorder whether the symptoms involve distressing emotional feelings (such as tension, anxiety, body pain, etc.) or unpleasant mental symptoms (such as phobias, depression, unwanted thoughts, etc.).

Before discussing these three areas of difficulty we shall take up some other pertinent aspects of the subject of mental health.

CHAPTER TWO

COMMON QUESTIONS ABOUT
MENTAL HEALTH

**Can we expect to have perfect peace at all times as a result
of becoming a Christian?**

THE ANSWER IS NO. Today there exists some confusion as to how many benefits one can expect from Christianity. Some Christians unrealistically hope to receive a cure for every physical, psychological, and spiritual problem that arises. Nowhere in the Bible has God promised relief from all our troubles in the present life, although it is true that in the future heavenly life he will give us freedom from pain and unhappiness (Rev. 21:4).

On the contrary, God has promised the Christian that in this life he will have a certain amount of tribulation (John 16:33; II Tim. 3:12). Christians are subject to accidents, physical diseases, psychological disorders, and pressing troubles, just as others are.

Then exactly what advantages are there in becoming a Christian, as far as our everyday life here on the earth is concerned? There are many. The Christian has a loving God and heavenly Father who is ready to give help to any Christian who asks Him (Heb. 4:16). He also has a King-Priest on the throne in heaven, God the Son, who "ever liveth to make intercession for them" (Heb. 7:25). In other words, a Christian has problems but he also has a source of help for his problems that non-Christians do not have. In fact problems offer an opportunity for direct application of the practical, everyday benefits of being a Christian.

13

Notice that God promises to help us, but does not promise to directly remove the problem or cure the disease. He may give us guidance to go to a doctor or a counselor who can help us get rid of the problem, or He may give us grace and strength to endure the hardship.

The Apostle Paul at times was "sorrowful, yet alway rejoicing" (II Cor. 6:10). Paul suffered want, yet he learned as a Christian to accept whatever circumstances he was in (Phil. 4:11-12). He managed to achieve some degree of peace of mind in his situation as he received help from God, who enabled him to be content (Phil. 4:13).

As it was pointed out before, even Christ did not have perfect peace of mind at every moment of His life, and was at times "distressed" (John 11:33, 38; 13:21; Matt. 26:37-39; Mark 14:33-34). We must accept the fact that in this life we will have distressing problems. But as Christians we also can expect God to help us either resolve or endure the problems (I Cor. 4:9-13; 12:9; Heb. 4:16).

Is psychological conflict abnormal or sinful?

The answer is no. One must first understand what a conflict is. When a person wants to do two or more things, and to accomplish one means to block another, that is a conflict. For example, a wife wants to do the grocery shopping at 3 P.M. But she also wants to attend a lecture at 3 P.M. on the same day. Since she wants to do both of these things and obviously cannot do both, she has a conflict.

A conflict, because it involves a failure to gratify a wish or need, usually produces frustration and tension. Everyday life is full of ordinary conflicts that a person resolves by giving up one wish for the sake of another. By giving up hope of gratifying one of the conflicting wishes, he relieves some of the frustration and clears the way for gratification of the remaining wish. This process is entirely normal.

Christ had conflicts just as any human being would have. One of His greatest conflicts resulted from His wish to obey God the Father and be crucified as opposed to His wish to avoid the horrible experience of dying on the cross (Matt. 26:37-39). He resolved it by deciding to obey God the Father.

What leads to abnormality is the putting off of the resolution of the conflict in any way. If one of the wishes is not abandoned the conflict ends in a deadlock and the feelings of frustration and tension continue, eventually giving rise to symptoms of nervousness. And it is no solution to bury the conflict in the subconscious, as this only results in continued or increased tension.

If one of the wishes involves wanting something impossible to obtain, then this too is considered abnormal, and only leads to unhappiness. A healthy way to resolve such a conflict is to relinquish an unrealistic goal in favor of a more realistic one. It is also abnormal to wish to engage in self-destructive or antisocial behavior, which always involves unjust treatment of others.

Conflict itself is not sinful. However, the conflict may involve wanting something that is sinful or forbidden. A person may think about doing that which is sinful. But there is a difference between thinking and lust which leads to doing. The biblical standard emphasizes what we do more than what we think (James 1:25-27; 2:24). Unbelievers will be judged by what they do—their works (Rev. 20:12-13). Christians will be rewarded in heaven on the basis of their works (I Cor. 3:13-15).

It is also true that our works stem from the thoughts and wishes of our mind (Prov. 4:23; James 1:15). Our mind is the battleground area—the place of conflict. If the battle in the mind is lost, then we fail, in that one of our thoughts gives rise to a sinful act.

God does not expect us to never have longings to do wrong. This is impossible for human beings. What He does expect us to aim for is the controlling of our thoughts and impulses so as to avoid, as much as possible, doing anything wrong. The achievement of this goal necessarily involves a struggle in the mind, or conflict.

The conflict should be conscious rather than subconscious so that the person can actively use all of his conscious knowledge and self-control in resolving the conflict. God expects us to be in conflict when we try to live a good Christian life (Rom. 7:7;

Gal. 5:17). We will continue to have these conflicts in the present life—they are a part of everyone's ordinary experience. When these conflicts begin to interfere with our adjustment to society, making us unhappy or ineffective, or resulting in suffering to others, then they should be resolved.

Is the biblical standard of behavior psychologically unnatural or unhealthy?

There is a widespread notion that the behavioral standard recommended by the Bible is unnecessarily severe, unnatural and contrary to sound psychological principles. This is absolutely not true. I have never found any command or exhortation in the Bible which, properly translated, interpreted, and applied, contradicts any psychological principle. Now, it is true that one can misunderstand and misinterpret the Scriptures and in this way claim that a biblical command is unsound. But here the fault lies in the misinterpretation. It is also true that one can leave the realm of psychological fact and claim as truth some unproven theory which may be contradictory to the Bible. But here the error is in claiming an unproven (and incorrect) theory to be fact.

Truth is truth wherever one finds it, and there is a hard core of truth to be found in the realm of psychology, the study of the mind. Truth in one area cannot contradict truth in another area. Therefore any behavior that is psychologically unhealthy is also scripturally unsound.

I will give two specific examples, sex and anger. Contrary to the beliefs of many psychiatrists and psychologists (and some Christians also), the Bible does not teach that sex is evil. It is not sex, but the improper use of sex that is wrong (that is, sexual relations with a forbidden sexual object). Hebrews 13:4 makes it clear that there is no moral defilement concerning sexual relations as such and that they are sanctioned by God within the limits of marriage. The marital partner is the ideal sexual partner, from both the biblical and the psychological standpoint.

Similarly, the Bible does not teach that anger itself is wrong. It is unjust, unreasonable anger or the use of improper forms for the expression of anger that is wrong. Ephesians 4:26 uses an imperative or a command to make it clear that God expects Christians to become angry—righteously indignant—when they have a justifiable reason to do so. The same passage also cautions us to stop committing sin in the way we express our anger. Some forms of expression of anger, such as murder, are unacceptable.

These two examples illustrate how many people become confused and say that sex and anger are condemned by the Bible. The Bible makes no such blanket condemnation of sex and anger. As we discuss different aspects of sex and anger later on in the book, I will show more clearly how the behavior recommended by the Bible is psychologically sound. It is a common tendency for people to interpret the Bible as more strict than it really is.

Every point of dispute will reveal on examination that the biblical standard is not unhealthy and that a true psychological principle is not unscriptural. As I discuss some psychological and spiritual principles later on in the book, this will be demonstrated.

Is there a set of spiritual rules that we can follow that will guarantee to eliminate any turmoil or sorrow in this life?

The answer is no. Some have a false idea that there is a list of rules one can follow and obey which will guarantee immunity from any mental unrest. No such set of rules exists.

However, I have summarized some guidelines for good spiritual and mental health in chapter 12 which, if followed, may bring freedom from much unnecessary worry and mental unrest. But even if a person followed all these suggestions, there would still be times when his peace of mind would be disturbed. Obedience to rules may enable the Christian to regain his peace of mind when it has been lost, but there is no way to entirely avoid the storms of life.

Sometimes a physical illness will cause a mental disturbance and the accompanying unrest, in spite of obedience to God. Or sometimes a satanic attack will cause a Christian to temporarily lose his peace of mind until he can muster his forces and take a positive stand against Satan.

Let me prove my point by reference to the life of the Lord

Jesus Christ. Certainly no one can accuse Christ of living in sin or of failing to follow the rules that produce good mental health. Yet in Mark 14:34 Christ said "My soul is exceeding sorrowful unto death." Matthew 26:38 confirms this by saying, "My soul is exceeding sorrowful." Furthermore, Mark 14:33 uses two other verbs to describe His reaction: "Sore amazed" literally means "terrifyingly amazed," and "very heavy" means "distressed." How could anything disturb Him that much?

Something here caused Christ to have turmoil and sorrow of soul rather than peace and joy. The explanation is that He was contemplating the horror of His coming death on the cross which would occur in a few hours. He had previously experienced a dread of this event and a struggle concerning it, saying, "Now is my soul troubled" (John 12:27). He naturally shrank from such an experience; yet, because he wanted to please God the Father, He subordinated His own will to the will of His Father. He prayed to the Father, "Not what I want but what you want!" (Mark 14:36, Williams). When He gave up His will and obeyed His Father's will, the struggle and unrest ceased.

We can definitely say that for every kind of problem that arises in a Christian's life, God has promised to provide grace in either removing the problem or making the burden bearable if it is not His will to remove it. Grace may involve the help that is available from a counselor or doctor.

If we live a psychologically sound, godly, and obedient life doesn't God promise us that we will experience less trouble?

The answer is both yes and no. Yes, in a sense we will experience less trouble if we live a psychologically sound, godly, and obedient life. God's full blessing will be upon our life. Such scriptures as I Peter 3:10-13 definitely teach that our life will be much better off if we are obedient. God expects us to mature emotionally into adulthood and to live a psychologically normal life.

On the other hand, Peter points out in the same chapter, verse 14, that even an obedient Christian may experience suffering.

Then he goes on to explain in verse 17 that suffering is not always chastisement for disobedience, but may be simply the will of God, perhaps in order to allow an exercise of faith on the part of His servant to bring about some other good purpose (Rom. 8:28). Of course "good" means good from God's viewpoint.

While it is true that the practice of evil brings tribulation and anguish (Rom. 2:9; I Tim. 6:10), it is also true that tribulation may come for other reasons to those who do not practice evil. Paul, in II Timothy 3:12, says that all who will (literally, "who want to") live godly in Christ Jesus will suffer persecution. Persecution frequently involves physical and mental suffering. But Paul exhorts the Thessalonians not to be moved (literally, deceived) in their afflictions, and points out that "we are appointed" unto these afflictions (I Thess. 3:3).

Why would God deliberately bring us tribulation, perhaps in the form of a physical or mental disorder, when we are living godly, obedient lives? We can summarize several good purposes:

1. To achieve purification of our Christian life (II Cor. 7:9, 11).
2. To produce patience (literally, "endurance") (Rom. 5:3; James 1:3).
3. To produce humility (II Cor. 12:7-10).
4. To produce dependence upon God (II Cor. 1:8-9).

These are obviously good reasons why God brings suffering into the lives of obedient Christians. Some of the godliest saints have had the most troubles. But their troubles have drawn them even closer to God.

A problem that does not have a disquieting or unsettling effect upon the soul is probably not a real conflict. In Mark 14:34 Christ said, "*My soul* is exceeding sorrowful." In II Corinthians 12:7 Paul said that he was *buffeted* by a messenger of Satan. Using the same word, Matthew speaks of the buffeting of Christ by the priests and elders who mocked Him and beat Him with their fists (Matt. 26:67). A ship that is being buffeted in a storm is being tossed around, beaten by the waves, bruised by the force of the water. Likewise, a Christian who experiences problems may find his soul greatly disturbed. But hope and great comfort are found in such Scripture verses as I Peter 5:10, where God promises to repair the damage after the storm is past. The words "make you perfect" in this verse mean to "repair."

When a Christian has a psychological disorder, is God, by direct intervention, the only one who can help? Or can legitimate help be obtained from psychiatrists or counselors in a way that is not unchristian?

The answer is that there are certain cases where the nervous Christian can be greatly helped by the aid of a counselor or psychiatrist who understands his particular problem and who knows what he needs.

Let me give an illustration. The menopause, or change of life, is a major cause of depression to some women. This period of transition for the woman may also be characterized by symptoms of fatigue and nervousness. She may cry easily, and even small problems may seem unsurmountable. It is unrealistic to expect God to remove these symptoms in a miraculous manner. This is a physical problem, although it may produce unfavorable manifestations in the spiritual and mental realm, and God has already provided remedies in the form of hormone pills, shots, and tranquilizing pills. There is no reason for God to directly intervene from heaven with a supernatural cure. He has already intervened by giving doctors the knowledge they need to relieve this physical problem.

It is also true that the Christian who is mentally disturbed due to spiritual factors may develop such severe physical symptoms in association with his mental problems that help in the form of physical remedies is necessary. For instance, the severely agitated patient who cannot sleep at all will become even more distressed and fatigued if he is not given some form of sedative to help him get a good night's sleep. In such a case the kind thing to do is to help him get some physical rest until his condition improves.

God has given to man a certain amount of knowledge about psychological matters. Man, by using this knowledge therapeutically, is able to help psychologically disturbed people. Why then do Christians feel it is necessary for God to offer help directly from heaven like a thunderbolt? Since God uses doctors to treat physical disorders and pastors, counselors, and Christian friends to help people with spiritual problems, why should He not also work through trained professional men to treat psychological disorders?

This does not mean that we should not also pray to God and have faith that He will help us. The question is what method will God use to help us. Some Christians err in claiming that as far as psychological disorders are concerned only God can help and only He is necessary. Yet, they admit that God works through people in physical and spiritual disorders. Why then are they so insistent that the psychologically disturbed Christian is making a mistake in seeking competent psychiatric treatment?

The reason sometimes given is that a non-Christian psychiatrist may lead the Christian patient astray morally. Although this danger may exist, a truly competent psychiatrist will not attack any sound moral principles. Furthermore, the treatment of many psychological problems does not even involve any Christian principles.

Another reason why some Christians are reluctant to go to a psychiatrist is that they tend to exaggerate the amount of benefits in the present life that are available in Christ. They want to claim a remedy for anything and everything. Such a feat would almost require magic. I remember one Christian who printed cards and passed them out in witnessing. Printed on the card were the words: "Christ has answered every need in my life." Yet the life of this man evidenced serious psychological problems. He was a glutton—dangerously overweight (in excess of 100 lbs.), and suffered from high blood pressure (as a result of being overweight). He died in middle age from a stroke, due to his high blood pressure. His claim that all his needs had been answered by Christ was nonsense. This man had tried to diet and lose weight but was always unsuccessful. He was driven to compulsive eating by his psychological problem for which he never sought psychiatric help.

Another reason that Christians avoid seeking professional help is that they are reluctant to admit that they have psychological problems. They would much rather call them "spiritual problems" and try to seek a cure through spiritual methods (such as prayer, reading the Bible, etc.). However, they are not facing up to the truth. We are told to recognize the truth and think upon it (Phil. 4:8; I John 1:7). If we have a psychological problem, then we should admit our need of psychological help, which may involve consulting another person.

I reject as dogmatic, rigid, and untrue any claim that God *always* or *never* helps a Christian with psychological problems through another person. To say "always" or "never" is to limit God unnecessarily. God can also help a Christian in response to self-examination, obedience, and faith. However, psychiatric therapy may be of great benefit to Christians in leading them to psychological maturity, which will then be reflected in more self-control and spiritual progress.

How can one tell the difference between a psychological and a spiritual problem?

Determining the difference between a psychological and a spiritual problem requires some knowledge, discernment, and experience. And frequently the two kinds of problems coexist, linked up together in some way. Here the answer is to separate them and apply the proper remedy to each separately. Often the spiritual problem is mainly a result of the psychological problem. In such a case, the resolution of the psychological problem may cause the spiritual problem to automatically improve. It can also work the other way. A spiritual problem can give rise to psychological symptoms, which in turn may disappear when the spiritual problem is resolved. As a help to the solution of these two interrelated problems, I have outlined below several different comparisons that can be made between them.

In chapter 10, section B, I have given a detailed outline as a help to recognizing evidences of psychological disorder.

Psychological Problems	Spiritual Problems
1. *The ability to think logically and to control the thoughts is decreased.* EXAMPLE: An illogical and unrealistic fear which the person does not want to have but which returns repeatedly, causing him distress. EXAMPLE: An impulse to rebel against God when the person earnestly desires to obey God.	1. *There exists a lack of desire to think properly, even though there is the ability to do so.* EXAMPLE: Thinking bad thoughts without becoming distressed about them. EXAMPLE: Not desiring to be willing to obey God, and deliberately rebelling against Him.
2. *Self-control is decreased so that repeated misbehavior results although there is a desire to behave correctly.* EXAMPLE: A person repeatedly misbehaves sexually even though he really tries to behave correctly.	2. *This involves the area of the will: misbehavior as the result of deliberate disobedience, and not from a lack of self-control. The individual is not sufficiently distressed by his spiritual failure.* EXAMPLE: A person who stubbornly misbehaves sexually because he wants to and has never determined in his mind to try to behave correctly.
3. *Conscience is frequently well developed or even too strict, causing normal or even excessive guilt.* EXAMPLE: Guilt may cause depression that interferes with one's mental ability to improve his behavior.	3. *Conscience may be underdeveloped, perhaps due to ignorance. Or person may ignore and reject the warnings of his conscience.* EXAMPLE: A person does not feel guilty enough to try to improve his actions; or, he may feel guilty, but represses his guilt and refuses to admit that he is violating his conscience.

Psychological Problems	Spiritual Problems
4. *Real motives behind misbehavior may be subconscious and require psychotherapy to bring them to the surface.* EXAMPLE: A person who misbehaves sexually, not out of sexual desire, but due to a subconscious longing for love and attention which was denied him in childhood. He tries to stop, but repeatedly fails.	4. *Real motives for misbehavior are usually conscious and the person may have to suffer unpleasant consequences before he becomes willing to change.* EXAMPLE: A person may not even try to stop misbehaving until he begins to suffer unpleasant results. He continues as long as he can get away with it.
5. *A problem is persistently unresponsive to the usual spiritual remedies (such as prayer, exhortation, etc.).* EXAMPLE: Spiritual failure continues to recur because the basic underlying psychological problem has not been resolved.	5. *When the proper spiritual remedy is appropriated the problem is solved.* EXAMPLE: A person's misbehavior ceases when he, as a Christian, adopts the proper spiritual attitude and relies on help from God. Exhortation from other Christians may help.
6. *A person is blind to the fact that he has a problem and repeated efforts to point it out to him meet with defeat.* EXAMPLE: A person cannot seem to "see" the problem because of a mental block. This is evidence of a subconscious reluctance to admit the truth.	6. *A person is ignorant but can see his problem when he is given clear and sufficient spiritual instruction.* EXAMPLE: A person's problem may disappear when he learns and appropriates a new truth which relates to his problem.

Do spiritual remedies cure a psychological disorder?

The answer is: "Not usually." Notice that I have used the word "do" instead of "can." It is granted that God is omnipotent and sovereign and can do anything He pleases. But He does not always choose to exercise these powers on our behalf. The issue here is really whether Christians have a right to expect God to cure their sicknesses in a way that bypasses His natural laws rather than working indirectly through men. God works through doctors to help our physical disorders, and through pastors, teachers, and Christian friends to help our spiritual disorders. Why, then, should He not also work through men to help us in relation to psychological disorders?

A person may develop a psychological disorder as the result of disregarding God's laws which govern the functioning of the mind. To cure the disorder, he must recognize and obey these psychological principles. The man who tries to ignore or rebel against God's laws concerning the body usually develops poor physical health. The same principle applies in the psychological and in the spiritual realm.

When we experience psychological distress God expects us to try to discover the cause and to do what we can to remedy it. Some Christians hopefully ask God to relieve these symptoms, yet they carefully avoid asking God to help them recognize the problem that is causing the symptoms. God expects us to be intelligent and to make use of whatever helpful truth is available, including information about psychological problems.

Because the causes of psychological distress are often subconscious, the help of another person is often necessary in discovering them. If a Christian requires the aid of a counselor or psychiatrist in recognizing the cause of psychological distress, this is not an indication that God has failed or that the Christian lacks faith. Problems are often buried in the subconscious where they are inaccessible, because they are painful to think about. One must bring them up to a conscious level before they can be dealt with.

Some Christians interpret various Bible verses to mean that we can expect God to intervene directly from heaven and help us with physical and psychological disorders. Some of these verses are given in chapter 4 along with the proper interpretation and application.

There is a "spiritual remedy" that does have profound psychological effects, and that is the experience of testing (Rom. 5:3; James 1:2-4). Testing can lead to maturity because the stress of suffering, whether it is physical or psychological, tends to weaken our personality habits. If a bad habit is weakened enough, then it becomes easier to do away with it and substitute a good habit in its place.

Bad habits do not easily go away; they tend to hang on tenaciously. Yet when a person experiences suffering, the habits lose their hold on him. The hidden (subconscious) motivations or feelings that lie beneath the habit are then exposed. The person becomes more consciously aware of the deeper problems within him that gave rise to and maintained his bad habit. By dealing with the problem consciously he can resolve it and thus eliminate the cause of the undesirable habit. Then by making a conscious effort to change and by asking God to supply the power, he can establish better personality habits.

Peter says, "he who has suffered in the flesh has ceased from [the enslaving habits of] sin, to the end that he might pass the remaining period of his life while in the body no longer [in slavery] to the lusts of men but rather [in submission] to the will of God" (literal, expanded translation of I Peter 4:1-2). In studying the life of Peter it is easily seen that he was often impetuous, sometimes foolhardy, and lacking in psychological maturity. There is no doubt that the Apostle Peter experienced suffering before he wrote his first epistle under the inspiration of the Holy Spirit. Because of his own example of suffering Peter was able to strengthen his brethren, as Christ had predicted he would (Luke 22:31-32). In I Peter 5:10 Peter writes that after the trial is finished, God comes along and restores us. The words "make you perfect" are properly translated "repair." After the storm is over, God repairs the damage.

In this way God can help us change for the better without our resorting to formal psychiatric therapy. Yet God's method of testing us does not violate or bypass His psychological laws which regulate the function of the mind.

God may also directly intervene in a situation where a Christian has no help available from any other person. A missionary who is isolated from other people and in severe psychological distress, not understanding his own problem, could only turn to God Himself for help. In such a case God may either help him tolerate the psychological stress and persevere, or He may miraculously relieve the symptoms at that time. But God *usually* works through ordinary, accepted methods, such as counseling or psychotherapy, in helping Christians that suffer from psychological distress.

Yet many Christians still insist that God will remove psychological disorders if they merely pray and wait to be cured. Such persons usually persist in this unrealistic view because they do not want to face up to the causes of their symptoms, namely the problems within themselves. They will not seek help from a counselor, for he might discover the truth, which they are not willing to face. But God wants us to think upon the truth (Phil. 4:8), and to walk in the light (I John 1:7).

In conclusion, spiritual remedies are for spiritual problems, while psychological disorders are usually best approached through counseling, psychotherapy, and other distinctly psychological approaches.

When a person becomes a Christian, are all the consequences of past sins removed?

The answer is no. We must realize that God has passed and enforces a law which says: "Whatsoever a man soweth, that shall he also reap" (Gal. 6:7).

Now God promises salvation from the penalty of sin and deliverance from eternal death in hell to everyone who receives the Lord Jesus Christ as his Saviour (Rom. 4:5-8; 5:1; Isa. 53:5-6). We are saved from "wrath" through Christ (Rom. 5:9). But only in the future life in heaven does God promise that we will be removed from the presence of sin. In heaven we shall be sinless

like Christ (Rom. 8:29; I Cor. 15:52-53; Phil. 3:21; I John 3:2).
But as long as we are in the presence of sin we must suffer the
consequences of sin—corruption and disease and trouble in this
life on earth.

This truth is made clear in the formation of bad habits. A man
may spend the first forty years of his life as a non-Christian, during which time he develops numerous bad habits. He may become accustomed to cursing, lying, and cheating. He may develop a terrible temper or become an alcoholic. When he is con-
verted to Christianity at the age of forty, his position is changed
immediately. While he was once outside God's family, he has now
become a child of God (John 1:12). But what has happened to
all his bad habits? He still has them. He begins to change these
sinful habits, but this is a gradual process and it will be years
and years before he can completely rid himself of these undesirable habits which he developed and cultivated before he became
a Christian. Although some of his bad habits may drop off right
away, others will require a struggle to get rid of them. Because
bad habits produce sin and he sowed and cultivated them for
forty years, he will reap some fruit from the habits even though
he has become a Christian.

Getting rid of bad habits involves both a human struggle and
the power of God. These habits will continue giving rise to sin
until they have been eliminated. And unless that sin is handled
properly, it will damage the soul. Peter warns that "fleshly lusts
. . . war against the soul" (I Peter 2:11). When a man's soul has
been damaged by sin for forty years, the effects of this damage
will not be erased overnight. By confession (see I John 1:9) he
can prevent any further damage until he has rid himself of his
sinful habits. But the damage already done to the soul is a handi-
cap to the process of gradual improvement.

This principle of reaping what we sow is an important factor
in nervous disorders. When we violate psychological and spiritual
laws we are bound to reap unpleasant consequences. As we become more obedient to these laws, and thus stop sowing, we will
eventually be able to stop reaping.

This concept has disturbed some Christians who feel that it

takes something away from the redemption we have in Christ. This is not so. There are many sins which, although forgiven by God, may result in unpleasant consequences. In the case of an ex-convict I know who became a Christian, he asked God to forgive his sins, yet he continued to reap at least two unpleasant results for a long time. One was the lowered self-esteem he experienced; he was ashamed of his past and it decreased his self-confidence. Second, people in general were suspicious of him and he sometimes had trouble holding a job after people found out that he had been a convict. He was forced to reap what he had sowed, in the sense that his earthly life was affected in an unpleasant way by what he had done. To expect this not to be distressing to a person is unrealistic.

CHAPTER THREE

THE PROPER ATTITUDE TOWARD PROBLEMS

IT IS OBVIOUS that our attitude toward a psychological problem is important. Many Christians are bewildered and discouraged by the fact that they have problems, attributing them to sin. Some are resentful against God for letting such unpleasant things happen to them. Others may be ashamed of their problems and put off going for treatment. These attitudes may be eliminated if we think of problems in the proper light.

They are part of the consequences of being human

It is only human to have some psychological problems. The whole human race is subject to physical, psychological and spiritual disorders. How did man develop this susceptibility? First there is the matter of Adam's original sin. As a result of this sin Adam (and thus the whole human race) became subject to the process of deterioration involving physical disease and culminating in physical death (Gen. 3:19; 5.5; Rom. 6:23; I Cor. 15:21-22). The race also became subject to certain calamities of nature, such as thorns and thistles in the ground interfering with the growth of crops.

In the civilization that subsequently developed from Adam and Eve, there occurred another failure of the human race. This is the failure to render to God the worship and honor which belongs to Him (Rom. 1:21-23, 25). Because men chose to render honor and give worship to others (creatures, images, idols) rather than

God, He chose to chastise mankind. As an act of judgment God "gave them up" (vv. 24, 28) to sexual perversion (vv. 24-27) and a reprobate (literally, "disapproved") mind resulting in their practicing those things which are not proper (v. 28). The term "reprobate mind" may refer to a mind which does not function properly. The specific practices which he refers to in verse 28 are enumerated in Romans 1:29-32. All of these acts are sinful, yet all of them are also symptoms of psychological disorders.

Thus the human race became subject to a vast host of psychological disorders, the study of which constitutes the field of psychiatry today. Sexual perversion is a result of psychological and/or physiological causes. Also such symptoms as extreme hatred and murderous urges in adults frequently stem from psychological problems. But our susceptibility to these disorders is a result of the failure of the human race to render God proper worship. This does not mean that everyone will develop all of these symptoms. But it does mean that we all are susceptible to them, given the right amount of psychological trauma and stress and/or physiological disorder.

Becoming a Christian does not bring freedom from the unpleasant experiences of ordinary human life, such as accidents, illnesses and other distressing circumstances. God has promised freedom from such things in the future life, but not in the present (John 16:33). So if we have psychological problems it is only an indication that we are human and therefore subject to the same problems that others have.

They are from God

Since God sovereignly regulates the lives of all Christians, not permitting anything to happen which may not result in "good" (Rom. 8:28), then in a sense it is true that we have a psychological problem because God has permitted us to suffer in this way. If God had wanted to prevent it, He could have. These good things mentioned in Romans 8:28-30 involve some situations that produce distress, unhappiness, sorrow, and turmoil. Although they are unpleasant, they are also good because of the effect they are designed to produce (II Cor. 12:7; I Peter 1:6-7; 4:19).

It is granted that everyone wants to eliminate the suffering such problems entail. Since such suffering constitutes a trial, we should not despise the trial, nor faint under it (Heb. 12:5), but rather be exercised by it (v. 11), and endure it as long as God feels it is necessary (Heb. 12:7; James 1:12). Then we can reap the profit from it which God intended (Heb. 12:10-11).

Thus the Christian who is suffering from a psychological disorder should realize that it is ordered by God and try to find out why. What lesson does God want him to learn? What does God want changed?

We bring them on ourselves

We must realize that when we fail to live a life consistent with good psychological principles we will always reap unpleasant consequences. This is true in the physical, psychological and spiritual realm. In this sense, we bring our troubles on ourselves. It is our own attitudes which are incorrect or unrealistic or illogical. The person who is disliked by everyone may bring this upon himself by his unfriendly behavior. The person who tries to handle a strong emotional feeling in an unhealthy way is bound to develop distressing symptoms as a result. It is all too easy to blame our troubles on other people, or to say it is only testing, and avoid recognizing our own failures. We are at least partly to blame for many of our problems.

Peter, an authority on suffering, wrote that there is no glory when a person is buffeted (literally, beaten with the fists) for his own faults (I Peter 2:20). The word *faults* here is a present participle of the verb *hamartanō*, which means "to miss the mark; to make a mistake through negligence." The Christian who is negligent in obeying the rules can expect to suffer for his lack of obedience. But this is his own fault, not the fault of others. He cannot explain his suffering by saying, "God is testing me," or "Others are persecuting me because I'm a Christian," for his suffering is brought on by his own mistakes. We need to take a look at ourselves and see what we have done or failed to do that contributed to the development of our distress. We need to examine ourselves.

They are opportunities for psychological and spiritual maturation

Although God could remove us from the storms of life, He has not chosen to do this. He permits trials in the life of every Christian and for a good purpose. It is the stress of a trial that will bring to the surface a psychological problem previously unrecognized. The symptoms of psychological distress point to some cause, perhaps a psychological problem. Here is an opportunity to try to discover what the problem is and correct it. Resolution of a psychological problem always results in greater mental health and often makes possible increased spiritual growth.

The Christian who properly faces a trial usually experiences a change in his heart attitude, and is transformed to a certain extent. If he has struggled with doubt and impatience, and has prayed and waited upon the Lord, he will find that eventually he will be able to master his problem (II Cor. 12:9; Phil 4:13). When the Christian recognizes this help from God as a manifestation of His power it results in glory to God as well as a change in the Christian's life. So suffering offers an opportunity to change for the better by resolving our psychological problems and transforming us by God's power and glory.

The question of cure or relief

What about a Christian who has a psychological problem with distressing symptoms which show no improvement? Just as cancer cannot always be removed, sometimes a distressing external situation cannot be eliminated. And sometimes a psychological problem may be inaccessible or incurable. What can one reasonably expect from God in such a situation? God gives grace to endure that which cannot be removed, but we must determine whether the problem can be eliminated or not.

God will usually do one of three things: (1) He may directly help the person develop insight as to why he is having trouble through self-analysis. This insight is frequently related to a trial or testing which exposes a problem previously unrecognized. (2) He may help indirectly by making it possible for the person to seek professional advice or treatment from someone else, such as a pastor, counselor, or psychiatrist. This is usually the best course to follow, provided a competent and trustworthy person is available for help. Or, (3) He may help the person tolerate the symptoms caused by the problem. In II Corinthians 12:7 Paul speaks of his thorn in the flesh, a weakness or infirmity which God would not resolve in answer to Paul's prayer. God instead chose to give him grace to withstand it (v. 9). Similarly we are encouraged by God to go to Him in prayer and ask for help in enduring the effects of our problems (Heb. 4:16).

In I Corinthians 10:13 we are told that we will not be tested in a way that is so great that we cannot bear up under it. (This verse is discussed in the next chapter.) But keep in mind that this endurance is somewhat dependent upon our obedience. A way out may exist but the Christian may not utilize it or even know about it. Also we must realize that a nervous breakdown may still be the best possible way to expose and deal with a psychological problem. A Christian who has a breakdown may not seem to have endured, but if he comes through the experience a healthier person psychologically and spiritually, then in a sense he did endure the problem. He survived the experience and profited from it.

God will either help us deal with our problems or will help us endure to the extent consistent with His plan for our lives.

It is unrealistic for any Christian to expect God to magically remove a psychological problem that is buried in the subconscious mind, or to permanently remove the symptoms of such a problem through faith and prayer. He has never promised such miraculous cures in the present life. This would be like expecting God to cure appendicitis without a doctor.

CHAPTER FOUR

PROBLEM VERSES

So FAR I have tried to present some basic facts of psychology and also refute some unrealistic ideas held by some Christians. In attempting to clarify these issues I must deal with several verses which are commonly misinterpreted and misapplied. Some people try to use these verses in an effort to prove the claim that God does as a general rule cure physical and psychological disorders through faith and prayer, without the aid of another person, such as a doctor. Therefore it is necessary to properly interpret these verses so as to discover what they do teach.

The Christian, in studying the Scriptures, should guard against the tendency to find what is not there. We are not to limit the Word of God, but neither are we to claim things for it that it does not teach. In interpreting a verse it is very important to consider the context, as this frequently governs the proper interpretation.

GALATIANS 5:16: "This I say then, Walk in the Spirit, and ye shall not fulfil the lust of the flesh."

Some think this verse suggests that if one walks by the Spirit then the problems stemming from the flesh (that is, the human nature) will be avoided. They say that if a Christian walks by the Spirit, then he could not possibly experience anything such as a mental disorder because such disorders come from our fleshly (human) nature.

The word "walk" is generally taken to mean "behave" or "conduct yourself." We are to "be conducting ourselves" by the Spirit.

Moreover, the verb is present tense, suggesting either a continuous action or a habitual one. To do this continuously, without any interruption, is impossible, because no one is perfect. Therefore, "Be habitually conducting yourselves by the Spirit" is probably a more legitimate rendering.

The word "by" ("in" in the King James version) is not in the Greek text. The translators have added this word to try to communicate the idea of the Greek dative case. If this case was used for indicating "sphere" (walk in the sphere of the Spirit), then it would mean: "Behave within the limits of [that is, marked off by] the Holy Spirit." However, if the case was used to indicate "means" (walk by means of the Spirit), then it would mean: "Conduct yourselves with a conscious attitude of dependence upon the Spirit [to provide the guiding and enabling power for your behavior]." Which does it mean? Here is one instance where our interpretation of a word influences our translation. Perhaps Paul had both concepts in mind. When one follows the Spirit in obedience, this implies that he is also depending on the Spirit for guidance. The trust and the obedience go hand in hand. However, most likely Paul meant *sphere:* "Behave the way that the Spirit wants you to."

Now the verse says that if we obey the Spirit then we will not fulfill the lust of the flesh. What is the meaning here of the word "fulfil"? The lust of the flesh may be considered something demanded of the person by his fleshly nature. When he gives in to and obeys his sinful nature then he is fulfilling this demand. But if he depends upon and obeys the Holy Spirit, he will not fulfill these demands of the flesh.

This does not mean that the flesh ceases to make these demands. Nor does it mean that these demands do not produce a conflict within the man (Gal. 5:17). Symptoms (such as tension and anxiety) may appear in his life even though the demands of the flesh are not being fulfilled. So this verse does not promise that walking by the Spirit eliminates all symptoms of mental distress stemming from the human nature. But it does promise that habitually walking in the sphere of the Spirit will produce outward behavior that is predominantly spiritual rather than fleshly.

Another fact to remember is that God does not offer us perfection in this life. Except for Christ, no one ever perfectly walked by the Spirit. Thus no one except Christ ever succeeded in not once fulfilling the lusts of the flesh. Only He was completely filled (controlled) by the Spirit (Eph. 5:18). Filling by the Spirit implies enough control so that the outward behavior is of a spiritual nature, but it does not imply that the old (human) nature is thereby rendered completely inactive. That would amount to a state of sinless perfection which is not possible in this life.

Moreover, a mental disorder reduces one's ability to walk by the Spirit. A person torn asunder by deep psychological conflicts and problems is not able to walk by the Spirit as he should until he has resolved his psychological problems and can exercise the normal amount of self-control.

II TIMOTHY 1:7: "For God hath not given us the spirit of fear; but of power, and of love, and of a sound mind."

Some believe this verse implies that since God gives us the spirit of a sound mind, there is absolutely no excuse for a Christian to ever have an unsound mind (that is, a mental disorder). Such persons accuse Christians who do suffer from mental disorders of being sinful and completely responsible for their own condition.

Before looking at the verse itself, such a view can be easily refuted. When a mental disorder stems from a physical disease process involving the brain, the patient is usually a helpless victim and is not responsible in any way for bringing on his disorder. Also many mental disorders stem from emotionally damaging experiences suffered in early childhood, when the small child could not be expected to know and respond correctly. Some children are victims of the meanness and cruelty of their parents. These children may grow up emotionally disturbed as a result of maltreatment by mentally disturbed adults. The fact that emotionally damaging experiences leave their psychological scars is irrefutable.

Now, to look at the verse, it is evident that the context of this book is an exhortation to hold to orthodox Christianity in the

face of persecution and a growing spiritual failure on the part of
the general Christian population (II Tim. 1:8; 2:1, 10, 15; 3:12;
4:5). So Paul tells Timothy not to falter, but to keep on exer-
cising the gifts of his ministry (II Tim. 1:6). Then in verse 7
he gives Timothy a reason why he should not falter. In effect
Paul says that fear (literally, cowardice) does not come from
God, therefore it comes from us. Paul does not say that Christians are never cowardly, but he does say that cowardly behavior
comes from the person, not from God. To contrast this Paul points
out what does come from God and lists power, love, and a sound
mind. His exhortation is to be brave and intelligently courageous.

From this verse one can only conclude that God the Holy
Spirit works in the life of a Christian to produce a sound mind
rather than an unsound mind. The spiritual life set forth by the
Bible is a psychologically healthy life. But the human nature is
still there and produces its own manifestations. Every Christian
is a mixture of what God is doing in him and what the person
himself is doing. In other words, the old human nature is not
eradicated in this life.

Moreover, the word "sound" emphasizes the concept of good
sense, especially the self-control necessary to carry out that which
is sound. It is the opposite of foolish. A person can have good
sense and yet suffer from a psychological disorder at the same
time which produces unsound thoughts and behavior. Obviously
this verse does not prove that Christians cannot have mental disorders.

PHILIPPIANS 4:11, 13, 19: Philippians 4:11 says: "Not that I am
speaking in regard to want. For I have learned in what [that is,
in whatever circumstances] I am to be contented" (literal translation.) This is taken by some to indicate that Paul learned to
have a happy frame of mind all the time, no matter what was
happening. Such people advance the idea that all Christians can
learn to be content, no matter what happens to them. Since an
emotionally disturbed Christian is not content, they assume that
such a person is not spiritual or is failing to properly appropriate
God's blessings.

Philippians 4:13 says: "I can do all things through Christ which strengtheneth me." This verse is claimed by many to support the idea that "all things" includes psychological problems and therefore a Christian can rid himself of any type of psychological problem or mental disorder by turning only to God, without seeking professional help. "I can do all things" is interpreted as including: "I can get well without any sort of professional help from another human being (such as doctor or psychiatrist or pastor)." Such a Christian, instead of seeking psychiatric help or pastoral counsel regarding a psychological disorder, would try to pray and have faith, expecting God to miraculously make the problems go away.

Philippians 4:19 is taken by many to imply the same idea. It reads: "But my God shall supply all your need according to his riches in glory by Christ Jesus." Some people interpret this to mean that if we have a psychological disorder causing us distress and/or spiritual failure, then we have a need which God is obligated to remove. Moreover, they assume that God should answer this need only through Christ, not through a process of psychotherapy, the use of a tranquilizer, or the helpful efforts of another person.

Such ideas do not represent correct interpretations or applications of these two verses. In chapter 2, I have already discussed some of the reasons why such ideas are not valid. Let us now look closely at these two verses and see what they do teach.

In verse 11 the context is clearly concerned with financial or material needs. In verse 10 Paul rejoiced that they had provided material help for him on his missionary journey. In verse 12 Paul talks of how at times he has had plenty, yet at other times he went hungry. What Paul was emphasizing was: "I have learned how to be content whether I have a shortage or an abundance of material things." So from the context we should assume that Paul had in mind the task of learning to be content in the midst of distressing external circumstances. He was not thinking particularly of one's inward emotional problems.

Paul also had in mind circumstances that could not be changed. God does expect us to improve our external circumstances if we can. But inward emotional problems also create discontent, and

God expects us to grow into emotional maturity. Any psychological problems creating discontent should be faced up to, and an attempt to resolve them should be made on a conscious level and in a healthy manner. It is also true that emotional problems reduce one's normal ability to adjust to unpleasant external circumstances. Although Paul does not mention it here (because it does not fit in with the point he was making) I am sure that he recognized that the more mature a person is emotionally the better he can adjust to distressing circumstances. A lack of maturity hinders one's adjustment to life, even though God's help is available.

But this does not completely settle the problem of this verse. For some will say that it establishes the general principle that a Christian should learn to be content in any sort of unpleasant situation. I do not believe this is a valid principle as stated above. It must be modified by several other important factors.

First we must define what the word "content" means. In our language today it means "satisfied" or "happy." But to properly interpret the verse we must determine what Paul meant by the word. The word is *autarkeia*, meaning, literally, "soul-sufficiency." It is used three times in the Bible (II Cor. 9:8; Phil. 4:11; and I Tim. 6:6). At the time Paul wrote, two thousand years ago, "content" referred to the ability to be independent of external circumstances, or self-sufficient. It referred to a settled state of mind. The word "resigned" is close to the meaning; but the word "happy" goes too far. We can picture Paul being beaten and tortured (II Cor. 11:23-25) and being resigned to his suffering. Yet he wasn't *happy* in the midst of being beaten. Rather he was sufficiently satisfied that he could continue his ministry in spite of the persecution.

It must also be remembered that even though Paul had God's power to help him, it took time, perhaps years, for him to learn to be content. This involved setting aside the gratification of some of his ordinary human needs and wants, and learning to tolerate a large amount of frustration. Any time needs are not satisfied, frustration results, and he had to become willing to get by with only minimal satisfaction of his basic human needs.

That brings up a third point. Just how deprived a life can a Christian live and still avoid experiencing acute unhappiness or a nervous breakdown? When too many basic needs are not satisfied over too long a time anyone will become depressed. For example, a wife who has a brutal, alcoholic husband who repeatedly abuses her and her children physically and mistreats her psychologically can hardly be expected to be content. God does help us to keep going in frustrating situations, but only up to a limit.

In the fourth place, God sometimes uses circumstances to produce discontent within us for the purpose of leading us elsewhere. The Christians in the early Jerusalem church were persecuted (Acts 8:1), and as a result many were discontent and left these distressing circumstances. They moved to other regions of the Roman Empire, where they preached the gospel (v. 4). But this was God's plan; He used the distress of persecution to cause them to move out evangelizing. Perhaps God wants a wife to leave a husband who is a brutal alcoholic. In such a case God's will would be for the wife to take steps to change her circumstances instead of trying to learn to be content with her situation.

Notice the context of Philippians 4:13, which has to do with Paul's experiences of suffering while engaged in his Christian career (see vv. 11-12). At times he had plenty of money; at other times he went hungry. Yet, he learned to be content no matter what his circumstances were. "Content" does not necessarily mean free of any frustration, irritation or distress. Rather it means accepting what we cannot change. In verse 13 Paul is saying, "I have power for [or, 'to do'] all things in Him who is strengthening me" (literal translation). What was in Paul's mind? "Having power [to do] all things" meant being able to go through all the unpleasant circumstances that he faced as a Christian without allowing them to hinder his ministry. "All things" is properly limited to "that which God might permit to happen to a Christian as a test or hardship to be experienced as a result of living the Christian life." It refers to those things that come our way through no fault of our own.

The "all things" does not refer to psychological distress brought on by a person's own failure to live a psychologically normal life. A person who rebels against God's laws governing the function of the mind must reap the consequences. The ethical and moral standard put forth in the Bible for the Christian to live by, properly interpreted and applied, is not a psychologically unnatural standard. To try to live in a way that conflicts with good psychological rules of health is not what God wants. In a sense, it is disobedience to God.

In verse 19 we find God supplies our *need*. If a psychological problem causes a spiritual failure, then we assume we have a need for the problem to be removed. From this verse, some Christians would assume that God in response to our faith and prayer, owes us a direct removal of the problem without help from other people. This is unsound.

Again we must notice the context to see what was in Paul's mind as he wrote. The word "but" is the Greek word *de* and is present also at the beginning of verses 15 and 18. It is a transitional word and implies that verses 15, 18 and 19 are all linked together and are related to what precedes in verse 14. In verse 14 Paul tells the Philippians that, even though he can endure financial stress, nevertheless they did well (that is, acted correctly) in sending him a gift of money. Then he gives three explanatory statements telling them why their giving was good. Each statement is introduced by *de* (see vv. 15, 18, and 19), which may be translated as "moreover."

Thus Paul had in mind his financial need and the Philippians' gift of money to meet that need. In verse 19 he indicates that their action in sending this gift was correct because, even if they subsequently developed a financial shortage themselves, God would provide for their needs also. He said, "You gave me what I needed. God will also give you what you need."

I will anticipate an objection: that such an explanation limits the Word of God. Some will argue that God is obligated to help us with our spiritual as well as material needs, for He encourages us to come to Him in prayer when we need help (Heb. 4:16).

My answer is that in verse 19 the primary emphasis is that of financial need, but that this can be applied as further proof of the general premise that God is able and ready to provide for all our needs. However, this premise must be modified by several other principles in God's Word. For instance, to be disobedient to God's laws, whether physical, psychological or spiritual in nature, brings consequences which must be endured. God cannot be expected to "help" us avoid the consequences of our own mistakes. God does not usually revoke His own laws just to relieve us from suffering. Moreover, there is much help available to the Christian that he never takes advantage of. God is not at fault when a Christian refuses to use the help that God has provided. A Christian who suffers from tuberculosis cannot blame God for failing to help him when he has refused to accept proper medical treatment from a physician. I feel it is useful at this point to again remind the reader that God usually works through people. Paul was refreshed spiritually by God, but it was through Onesiphorus (II Tim. 1:16). God can help us by working through a good psychiatrist to bring us into a more healthy state psychologically.

Moreover, this promise must be modified by the fact that the final decision about whether a need is really a need must be left up to God. We may feel convinced that we need something badly, yet God refuses to give it. But in God's eyes perhaps we did not really have a need. Paul thought he needed removal of his thorn in the flesh, but he was wrong. He really needed to keep the thorn so that he would not become too proud (II Cor. 12:7). This is why Paul can say that all things work together to produce a good result for those who love God (Rom. 8:28).

In summary, these verses cannot be used to support the idea that God habitually grants all our needs without the agency of human instruments and conformity to the natural laws governing the mind and body.

I CORINTHIANS 10:13: ". . . God is faithful . . . who will not suffer you to be tempted above that ye are able. . . ."

Some Christians say that this verse teaches that, since God has provided a way out of any testing, there is no excuse for any Christian ever failing to bear up. They assume that developing a psychological disorder or symptom indicates spiritual failure on the part of the Christian. Now I recognize the fact that sometimes a spiritual failure does result in symptoms of mental distress. Sometimes the Christian fails to appropriate the help from God which is available, either through ignorance or negligence. But this is not always the explanation.

Moreover, I do not believe that this verse, properly interpreted, refers primarily to Christians bearing up under stressful situations without breaking down. To understand what Paul had in mind when he wrote the verse we must study the context.

The context actually begins in chapter 9. In I Corinthians 9:24-27, Paul is exhorting Christians to run the race effectively, to maintain self-control; in other words, to strive to become and remain effective in their Christian life, so as not to lose their future rewards. Then in chapter 10 Paul expands on this subject and warns them about the danger of complacency. In verses 1-11 he says that our ancestors, the Jews, God's people, had many blessings and experienced great things as they walked with God. But they fell into sin and idolatry and God had to judge them. They thought they were secure, but something happened and they fell into sin and had to suffer chastisement. Paul warns that we should profit from their example and not make the same mistake (vv. 6, 11).

Then, in verse 12, Paul indicates the mistake they made. The word "wherefore" (AV) is *hōste* and could be translated "so then" or "as a result then." Paul warns, "Christian, you watch out lest you should fall into sin and idolatry as they did." The lesson is that it is dangerous to think that you have it made, because one who becomes complacent tends to relax his efforts at being a good Christian. This is just what Paul did not want them to do. In chapter 9, verses 24-27, Paul admonished them to keep pushing, keep fighting, and keep working, lest they become careless and fall into sin.

In verse 13 Paul makes an initial point that we all have to fight the same kind of temptations. His next point is that God sees to it that, when we are presented with a temptation: (1) It is not one that is so much greater than our spiritual achievement that we could not hope to meet it successfully; and (2) there is always a way out, so that we can resist the temptation and survive it without falling into sin.

Of course, the Christian may fail, through ignorance or negligence, to take the way out. The Bible gives us many instructions which, if followed, would result in greater success in living the Christian life. David, when he saw Bathsheba bathing, was tempted. He could have resisted the temptation, but instead he watched her (II Sam. 11:2), inquired about her (v. 3) and finally sent messengers to bring her to him (v. 4). Instead of taking the way out, he pursued the temptation. We are told to flee certain things (I Cor. 6:18, 10:14; I Tim. 6:11; II Tim. 2:22) rather than stay and fight them out.

Paul refers in I Corinthians 10:13 to the Christian duty to meet temptation without falling into sin. The verse is not concerned with our bearing up under testing without mental distress. It is true that the word *peirasmos* can mean either testing or temptation. However, the context of this verse is the danger of falling into sin and idolatry in ordinary temptations, by not meeting the Christian standard of behavior in everyday life. The context is not that of maintaining one's mental health under the stress of trying situations or inward psychological problems. Therefore, my judgment is that the verse refers to avoiding sin, not avoiding symptoms of mental illness.

JAMES 5:14-15: James 5:14 begins: "Is anyone among you sick?" The rest of the verse seems to recommend calling an elder instead of a doctor and substituting faith and prayer and anointing with oil for the appropriate treatment for the disease. Verse 15 goes on to claim that "prayer marked by faith" will save (that is, make well) the sick. Verse 16 urges confession of sins and prayer so that they may be healed (*iaomai* means to heal a disease).

Some people point to these verses as proof that when a Christian is sick, physically or psychologically, he has only to turn to God in faith and prayer and God will heal him. They would claim that turning to doctors or psychiatrists is going contrary to the scriptural way.

These verses raise several problems of interpretation and application. Rather than avoid the issues they raise, I feel it is important to try to determine what legitimate conclusions can be drawn.

First we should look at the words themselves. In verse 14 the word "sick" is *astheneia*, "a weakness, sickness." It is the same word used of the sickness of Lazarus (John 11:14), and of those sick that the disciples were commanded by Christ to heal (Matt. 10:8). In those days elders commonly visited the sick, as pastors today still visit people in the hospital and frequently pray for the sick. The term "pray over him" refers to the stretching out of the hands in prayer over the sick one. The anointing of the sick person's body with olive oil was common at that time. Notice in Mark 6:13 that the disciples, sent forth on their mission of announcing Christ's arrival, "anointed with oil many that were sick, and healed them."

In verse 15 the phrase "save the sick" is properly rendered "make well the sick." The word "save" was frequently used in this sense. The phrase "The Lord shall raise him up" refers to being raised up off his sick bed. In verse 16 a more obviously medical word is used for healing: *iaomai* means "to heal"; *"iatros"* means "physician." This refers to the process of treating disease, ordinarily carried on by a doctor.

The first question raised is that of miraculous healing. Did it occur then? There is no doubt that it did. Christ healed, and delegated this ability to the disciples when He sent them out to announce His arrival (Matt. 10:1, 8). It is clear that their use of this ability was not to be for money (see Matt. 10:8-10), but was primarily for the purpose of attesting to the authority of the messengers and thus authenticating their message. The apostles also were given this gift to attest to their authority as God's messengers so that their message would be received as from God. (See Acts 9:32-35; 40-42.) Members of the first century church were given various gifts, and some received the gift of healing (I Cor. 12:9, 28, 30). But there were a number of gifts given to this early church which were not continued after the first century or so. Paul testified that the gift of tongues would cease (I Cor. 13:8). The purpose of any gift was always for the benefit of the body of Christ, the true church (I Cor. 12:7, 12, 21-25, 27). The early church, before all the New Testament Scriptures had been given and recorded, had need of some miraculous signs (such as tongues, prophecies of the future, and miraculous healings), not only as an encouragement to itself but also to attest to the authority and authenticity of its message to unbelievers. But once the New Testament (and thus the whole Bible) was completed, the need for such things dropped off. After this I do not believe that the Holy Spirit continued to grant gifts of tongues and healings.

Does miraculous healing occur now? This depends on how you define it. If you mean by this that God now gives some Christians a special gift of power which enables them to heal sick people in a miraculous manner, then I answer no. I do not accept as valid the credentials of some people who go about claiming to have this gift. The burden of proof rests upon them. However, I do not question that today God sometimes, in response to prayer, enables a sick person to recover, who apparently would die otherwise. But this is not the same as the gift of healing.

The question then hinges on this issue: when a Christian becomes sick, should he first of all turn to God and ask and expect Him to miraculously heal him of his physical or psychological disease? Or should he first turn to a trained doctor or professional person for help, at the same time asking God to bless and work through the doctor's efforts? The Bible gives a clear answer to this question. Christ Himself said that one who is sick needs a physician (Matt. 9:12). Christ recognized that physicians have a legitimate place in ordinary life: that of treating diseases, using whatever knowledge God has given them. Paul recognized Luke as a physician (Col. 4:14). Paul had the gift of healing (Acts 28:8-29), yet obviously he was not able to heal sick persons indiscriminately or at will. (See Phil. 2:27; II Tim. 4:20.) It is also unrealistic for the Christian to expect God to heal him miraculously when trained professional care is available.

Can God be expected to heal miraculously in cases where a doctor or medicine is not available? Today if a doctor is not available or if the doctor's treatment is not working, can a Christian turn to God on the basis of James 5:14-16 and expect God to heal him? The answer is: only sometimes. God will not usually heal miraculously. In most cases the Christian suffers the usual consequences of his disease process, which is operating according to God's laws. To see when a Christian might utilize the promise of James 5:14-16 we must look closely at these verses.

The anointing with oil was a routine procedure in the days of the early church. Early Christians used the rite; in fact, they never gave or took any medicine without anointing with oil. The oil was symbolical, perhaps of the need for the work of God the Holy Spirit, somewhat like the water used in the baptismal rite. The oil applied by the elders most likely signified their recognition of the need for God the Holy Spirit to bring about improvement, whether with or without the usual medicine.

In verse 15 we have a key phrase, "the prayer of faith." It is prayer characterized by faith that makes the sick well. This faith must be faith that "in this particular person with this particular illness on that particular day God will grant recovery." Thus the Christian must have received assurance that God will answer his prayer for recovery with a positive answer. Only then could such a prayer be characterized by faith and only then would it be followed by healing.

It is granted that perhaps in every illness the elders and the Christian might pray for recovery. But assurance of a positive answer would not be present each time. We all have prayed at times, asking for something but not knowing that it will be granted. This is the case when there is a supernatural assurance of a positive answer that these verses refer to.

In verse 16 it is only "effectual fervent prayer" (literally, "a supplication, when it energizes") that avails much (literally, has much force). This again calls attention to the unusual, out of the ordinary, nature of the prayer. Only the prayer of a person convinced, correctly so, by God, that the answer will be "Yes" can "energize." Any other prayer is only an expression of what the person wants, but has no assurance he will get.

Therefore I believe the proper application of this verse may be twofold: (1) That elders may legitimately pray over a sick Christian, asking God to bless the results of the ordinary medical treatment used; (2) also that in those times of crisis, when a Christian is sick but God has granted assurance that recovery will occur, elders may legitimately pray over the sick Christian, expecting God to heal regardless of what medicine has or has not been tried.

I believe the application must be modified by this principle: God expects the sick (physical or psychological) to routinely turn for help to those professional persons trained to treat such disorders, unless there is a definite problem which prevents this (such as lack of a doctor) and unless there is a special leading from God to use a prayer and faith approach. I am convinced that usually God intends for the psychologically sick Christian to seek psychological help (thus observing God's psychological laws) in treating his illness. The stubborn refusal of a Christian to admit he needs professional help in resolving his psychological problems and his insistence that "God and I can do it alone" (when God has not given any such special leading) must be interpreted as a resistance to change on the part of the person. Such resistance is unbecoming to the Christian, for he is obligated to keep his self, the vessel used by God, in the best physical and psychological condition possible, for most effective service for God.

CHAPTER FIVE

HEREDITY VERSUS ENVIRONMENT

HERE WE MUST TACKLE the problem of whether psychological disorders are inherited or are due to environmental stresses. I will not try to present a mass of data on this subject, but rather what I consider to be reasonable conclusions that can be drawn at this time.

There are certain specific diseases involving various parts of the body, including the brain, that are inherited. With these diseases come mental symptoms because of physical damage to the brain and/or biochemical abnormalities in the brain tissue. Although some of these conditions can be prevented by appropriate treatment, after they have developed and the damage is done, there is no real cure available.

Our interest here is more in what might be labeled a "nervous tendency." Can a person inherit the tendency to be nervous, or to be more vulnerable to developing a psychological disorder? Many doctors think so. Each person seems to be born with a certain amount of "innate capacity" to withstand the hard knocks of life. Since some have a greater capacity than the others, they can tolerate more psychological stress, without developing nervous symptoms, than others. Of course, when we refer to "innate capacity" we really mean one's "God-given capacity." God has established and continues to regulate, through His laws of heredity, this process by which a person inherits his physical and psychological characteristic tendencies.

Another more obvious way in which heredity plays a role in psychological makeup is in the matter of intelligence. A person born with a low IQ will usually experience more difficulty in handling life's problems than someone who is highly intelligent.

Unless a person inherited a definite disease or a very low IQ, the effect of his environment would usually be more important than the effect of his heredity. I have tried to summarize the different ways in which our environment acts upon us.

The experiences in life, both good and bad, during the formative years (from birth to 21 years), combine with the physical and psychological tendencies which were inherited to produce at maturity (theoretically, age 21) a completed personality. A personality may be strong and healthy, or weak and sickly, depending on what happened to the person during these years and how he responded to those events. He may be confident or insecure, cheerful or depressed, loving or hateful, trusting or suspicious, affectionate or cold, logical or illogical, as part of his basic personality.

Then, after entering adult life, he responds to those experiences that continue to occur in his life either in a healthy or an unhealthy way, depending on his personality. Many experiences produce psychological stress, such as: marriages, divorces, births, deaths, physical diseases and accidents, and financial losses. If his response to this stress is anything less than healthy or normal, then nervous symptoms will likely develop. In the matter of present environmental stress we would, of course, include such things as spiritual conflicts and anything that would upset us. In the chart below I have tried to outline the interrelationships between heredity and environment before and after childhood.

What then is God's provision for the Christian who seems to have inherited a tendency to be nervous? One must first admit that the tendency exists and not be ashamed of it, since apparently it was God's will for his life. When suffering arises, perhaps at least partly related to this nervous tendency, and we cast the problem in the lap of God, then what will He do about it? (I Peter 5:7). God will either reduce the nervous tendency, or He will give grace to help endure the suffering that results (II Cor. 12:8-10; Heb. 4:16).

It is unlikely that God very often removes an inherited con-

INHERITED CONSTITUTIONAL TENDENCIES		EFFECT OF ENVIRONMENT DURING THE FORMATIVE YEARS
(low or high IQ; neurotic tendencies; physical tendencies; etc.)	PLUS	(loved or rejected; treated well or mistreated; etc.)

COMPLETED PERSONALITY AT AGE 21

(mixture of mature and immature traits)

PLUS

EFFECT OF PRESENT ENVIRONMENTAL STRESS

(marriages; divorce; births; deaths; accidents; diseases; disappointments; financial stress; spiritual conflicts; etc.)

HEALTHY, APPROPRIATE, LOGICAL RESPONSES		UNHEALTHY, INAPPROPRIATE, ILLOGICAL RESPONSES
	OR	(resulting in nervous symptoms)

stitutional nervous tendency, since this would involve a violation of His laws of heredity. I do not say He never does it, but only that it must be rare. It is usually futile to ask God to do this. His answer is usually no. Instead He provides grace to enable us to endure any unpleasant consequences that may result from such a tendency.

Some keep on chafing and fretting about this tendency. They keep on begging the Lord to remove it even though He has said no. They never give up trying to find some way to get rid of it. These persons may be guilty of resisting God's will for their life. Peter describes this as a form of pride (I Peter 5:5). He seems to indicate that humility is a "patient acceptance of God's will." Peter points out that God gives grace to humble ones, that is, God enables those who submit to His will to endure the trials and problems that come into the life as a result of God's will. James also points this out (James 4:6).

But as for those who are not submissive, the proud ones, God sets Himself against them. Literally, God "ranges into battle against them." This is the translation by Lightfoot of the word "resist" in I Peter 5:5 (see also James 4:6).

Thus the remedy for a Christian prone to nervousness is to cast the problem into the lap of God and ask Him to solve it. God will give the Christian the grace to endure problems and let them become exercises of faith (Heb. 12:7, 11; James 1:12).

CHAPTER SIX

PHYSICAL CAUSES OF NERVOUS TENSION AND PSYCHOLOGICAL DISORDERS

THE WAY in which physical factors are involved in nervous symptoms is simple: Whatever affects the body also affects the mind. If the body is tired, then so is the mind. If the body is sick, then the mind is affected by the physical sickness.

These physical conditions in which the primary and most prominent manifestations involve the brain are called "brain syndromes." The symptoms may vary from mild nervousness up to severe disturbances of memory and intellectual ability, and bizarre psychotic symptoms. A person with a brain syndrome may be disoriented as to time and place; may show a poor memory; may show a disturbance of the usual intellectual functions (knowledge, learning, understanding, calculations); may develop poor judgment; may show inappropriate and/or poorly controlled emotions; may show neurotic or psychotic symptoms; and may, uncontrollably, become involved in misbehavior. He may develop delusions and hallucinations, and frequently seem confused.

It is very hard to fight successful spiritual battles and to make sound spiritual decisions when the body (and the mind) is weakened from physical causes. The simplest way to illustrate the physical factor is to discuss some of the different types of physical conditions which will produce mental manifestations.

54

Hereditary Diseases

Here are the diseases, mentioned briefly in the previous chapter, which are inherited. An example is phenylketonuria. This particular condition is an inherited biochemical abnormality resulting in brain damage during the early years of childhood. The diagnosis of this condition can be made in young infants. If these infants are kept on a certain type of diet for the first few years of their life, then the brain damage can be prevented.

Mental Deficiency

I have listed this as a separate factor because it is thought to be of physical origin rather than psychological. A person who is low in intelligence is less capable of dealing with any kind of problem in life. He is prone to become easily frustrated and nervous whenever he attempts something and fails. He suffers from low self-esteem and lacks self-confidence. He is not able to reason as effectively as a person of higher intelligence and thus is prone to misunderstand social situations. Misbehavior may result from his inability to understand or obey the laws of society.

Some cases of mental deficiency are inherited, such as Mongolism. Others are due to brain damage at birth, congenital abnormalities, or infection, as in meningitis. Epilepsy may also be associated with inherited mental deficiencies. Although many mental defectives can be trained to work at simple tasks and become self-supporting, there are no known cures for these conditions.

Physical Fatigue

The presence of fatigue is always a warning that the person's body and/or mind has been subjected to too much work or pressure, without enough rest and relaxation. A person who is trying to accomplish too many things too fast will become fatigued because of too much bodily activity. A person with a psychological disorder, suffering from nervous symptoms, may experience fatigue because his mind is working too much, constantly trying to get rid of his problems or symptoms. The following things are said to be productive of fatigue: overwork with too little rest and relaxation; boredom; loneliness; financial worry; domestic worry; psychological conflicts; constant frustration; bright lights; loud noises; constant pain; and bad weather. Physical diseases such as malnutrition, thyroid disease, low blood sugar, and chronic infections, such as brucellosis, may also cause fatigue.

Fatigue, when it develops, prevents the mind from being as efficient or as effective in coping with problems. A person who is fatigued may also be nervous and irritable. If a person works all day and fails to get enough relaxation or sleep, he will develop fatigue sooner or later. This fatigue may lead to some type of breakdown unless a proper balance of work, sleep, and relaxation is restored.

This is easy to see in the young housewife and mother who perhaps has had her third baby and now finds herself going around all day minding babies, fixing bottles, handling diapers, washing and ironing, doing housework, cooking meals and losing sleep at night. Her life frequently becomes unbalanced with too much work and not enough relaxation and rest. She tries to accomplish more and more work in one day's time, doing too many things too quickly, living under constant pressure, and then finds herself feeling tired. She is developing fatigue.

She goes to the doctor complaining of being tired and perhaps nervous. The doctor examines her, does a blood count, maybe checks her metabolism, and ends up finding no organic disease.

She is suffering from chronic fatigue, which makes her mind as well as her body feel tired. A tired mind cannot cope with the problems of everyday life effectively and so she becomes irritated by minor things that ordinarily would not irritate her. She has trouble concentrating her attention on anything. She loses her enthusiasm for the things she used to enjoy. She does not seem to feel the same love toward her husband. She develops a carelessness toward things about which she should be careful. She does not seem to think about God as much any more, or read the Bible and pray as she used to. "Am I backslidden?" she asks. The answer is probably no; she is not backslidden. She is fatigued and this has affected her mind. It is obvious that this same proc- ess is going on in many businessmen today who allow the pressures of business to crowd them into a daily schedule that is entirely too busy.

Remember that God the Holy Spirit in speaking to us as Christians works through our conscious mind. If our mind is fatigued and befuddled, then the Holy Spirit cannot get through to us as well as before. We cannot pray as we used to do because prayer is an exercise of the mind, and if the mind is tired, naturally we cannot pray as well.

The body and the mind are not made to be too busy; they do not thrive on pressure. There is a limit of stamina, which varies with individuals; this limit, when it is exceeded, puts a definite strain upon both the body and the mind. The body and mind carry this burdensome load for a time, but eventually, if the person does not slow down and relax, the body and mind develop fatigue, which forces the person to slow down. If he takes the body's hint and rests and relaxes more at this point, then the fatigue will disappear after a while.

If he ignores the warning symptom of fatigue, then eventually he will reach a point where his body and mind simply refuse to go on at that fast pace. At this point he may have what is commonly called a nervous breakdown (which is a somewhat vague term, but yet one which everyone seems to recognize). At any rate, the body and mind refuse to carry the burden any longer, and the person has to take a rest and get out from under the pressure because he becomes physically and mentally incapacitated.

Of course, when this happens, rest is just what he needs. After he has rested awhile he begins to improve. He will continue for a while to reap the results of the abnormal strain pressed upon himself, but in time the reaping process comes to an end and he gets well. This process of improvement usually takes place in some hospital or rest home or at his own home, where he is forced to do nothing but rest and relax, whereas he should have been resting properly in a balanced life all along, as a preventative measure.

The Lord Jesus Christ had to take time out occasionally to rest during His ministry here upon the earth, because He was truly human. As a man He felt the need of periodic rest and relaxation, away from the crowds of people to whom He ministered (Mark 6:31).

Sometimes, however, a person cannot avoid a time of heavy work and pressure. A college student, for example, often carries a heavy load in class, and in addition has to work for a living. He does not have time to relax as much as he should. The answer in his case is twofold. First he will have to pay the penalty for abusing his body and mind by overworking them. He will manifest the strain of this situation by developing fatigue. Such a period of overwork will cost him something. In addition he should be careful to follow each school period of work and study and pressure with a period of less work and more rest, to help him build up resistance against fatigue. A period of abnormally heavy strain ought to be followed by a period of unusually light strain. This will enable his body and mind to recover, and thus he can avoid a breakdown.

A breakdown results when there has been too much strain and pressure for too long a time, without enough rest. One cannot ignore God's laws of nature regarding the needs of our body and mind for rest and relaxation.

If the Christian works under such abnormal pressure and strain and develops fatigue, then he should immediately reconsider his decision as to what the Lord's will is about such work. The development of fatigue is usually an indication that the Christian has been trying to do more work than God has willed for him to do in that period of time. If you cannot work sixteen hours a day without developing fatigue, then it is very unlikely that God would lead you to work sixteen hours a day. When God's sustaining grace expires for that day and you become tired, then it is time to quit and rest instead of continuing your labor.

God does not lead Christians to abuse their bodies and minds with too much work. God wants us to take proper care of our bodies and minds as well as we know how. For it is through us, our bodies and minds, the vessels of God, that God works. If our mind is numb with fatigue, we are not capable of being used effectively by the Holy Spirit. So in regard to this factor of fatigue, the best thing to do is to avoid overwork by living a balanced life. If fatigue develops because of overwork, then the cure is to get more rest and relaxation. Let me issue a warning at this point. The Christian who lets himself become fatigued is asking for trouble. He offers Satan the ideal time to launch an attack. The Christian is not alert and on guard as he should be, and Satan can hit with great force without any warning. We always need to be in the best fighting condition possible.

Physiological Letdowns

What I have in mind is the situation that develops when there is a normal physiological slowdown of the whole body, which may be manifested in the mind by symptoms of tiredness or depression or similar symptoms. For instance, frequently when a woman is recuperating after having a baby, there is a period of a few days or a few weeks when she gets the blues. Has she backslidden? Is she in rebellion against the Lord? Is there unconfessed sin in her life? Probably not, because she is simply experiencing mental manifestations of a normal physiological process in her body. The body processes during pregnancy are speeded up. Then, after the baby comes, the body returns to a slower rate of activity. This readjustment is sometimes mentally disturbing. The same thing occurs frequently after an operation, or after a period of prolonged bed rest, when the body has become slowed down. Time and rest are usually all that is needed to clear up this condition. It also occurs in women during the menopause or change of life. Here the body is undergoing changes due to a decreased supply of female hormones within the body. A woman with this condition may be depressed and tired, and may become irritable and cry easily. She cannot handle life's problems as well as she used to; every molehill seems like a mountain.

The remedy is obviously medical treatment, either in the form of a tranquilizer or supplemental hormone medicine or both. This is the only thing that will relieve the symptoms. In most cases there is no reason why hormones or tranquilizers should not be given, and they will transform the condition of the patient mentally and physically. Many fine Christian women have suffered years of mental torture, living lives of what they call "spiritual defeat," always fighting some spiritual battle and usually losing, when what they really need is medication. Such a remedy would make new persons of them. Again in this type of case the patient should make use of the provision that God has made, and not expect God to work in a supernatural manner to give relief.

Destruction of Brain Tissue

Destruction of the brain tissue itself will produce mental symptoms. Infections such as syphilis of the brain, meningitis, and tuberculosis of the brain, as well as any damage to the brain as in a car accident, cause destruction of brain tissue. Any lesion which occupies space in the skull, such as a brain tumor, hemorrhage or abscess will also cause damage. The only cure, of course, is to treat the disease.

Decrease in Blood Supply to the Brain

Anemia or heart failure interferes with the amount of oxygen carried to the brain in the blood, producing symptoms of tiredness and sometimes depression. A very frequent condition that comes on with aging is that of hardening of the arteries. When this condition develops in those blood vessels carrying blood to the brain, it results in a decrease in the blood supply to the brain. This may produce mental confusion and other disturbing mental symptoms. The only remedy is to improve the blood supply whenever possible.

Disturbance of Biochemical and Physiological Balance

There are many complex biochemical reactions occurring in the brain all the time. Any disturbance in this system of chemical reactions may result in some mental symptoms. For example, an underactive thyroid gland creates mental apathy and depression while an overactive thyroid causes nervousness and tension. Any condition which affects the water and salt balance in the body may disturb brain function, such as: diabetes; severe kidney disease resulting in uremia; and severe vomiting and/or diarrhea. Vitamin deficiency may impair brain function. Attacks of low blood sugar (hypoglycemia) and brain infection (encephalitis) will produce nervous symptoms. The remedy for all of these disorders is the restoration of the person's physical condition to normal. When this is accomplished the mental symptoms usually disappear.

Improper Use of Chemicals and Drugs

The most common example of this type of disorder is alcoholic intoxication. A drunk person has an acute brain syndrome, his brain function is disrupted by alcohol. Consuming moderate to large amounts of alcohol over a period of many years may result in permanent brain damage, at which time the person will develop a chronic brain syndrome.

The same thing may happen with drugs. The most common offenders are: barbiturates; bromides; narcotics, such as opiates; and stimulants, such as dexedrine. The improper use of these drugs can result in severe mental disturbances.

Any poison taken into the body usually produces some mental symptoms. Examples are: arsenic; lead; mercury; and carbon monoxide poisoning.

Summary of Physical Factors

There are many kinds of physical factors that can play a part in nervous symptoms. In evaluating a particular patient a doctor must look for and correct any physical factor present before he can expect any real improvement in the mental condition. Frequently a particular case of mental disorder cannot be traced to just one cause. Often it is due to a combination of several factors which interact to produce a breakdown, or some other mental disturbance.

Christians frequently do not realize how much their spiritual outlook is affected by their physical condition. It is hard to feel and act spiritual when one is physically ill. So we must correct anything physically wrong with us in order to operate at the highest peak spiritually.

CHAPTER SEVEN

PSYCHOLOGICAL CAUSES OF NERVOUS TENSION AND PSYCHOLOGICAL DISORDERS

Theory of Human Behavior

ANY ATTEMPT to organize observations and data collected about human behavior should not be treated as a dogmatic, rigid system of truth. The data itself may be quite objective, but the system by which the data is collected, organized, and interpreted is only a matter of convenience. It is a subjective attempt to explain the meaning of the data and must be modified from time to time as more accurate data is acquired. Therefore the system must be considered a theory, true and accurate only to the extent of the reliability of the information.

The following theory of human behavior attempts to recognize the many motivating forces and needs in man, whether physical, psychological, social, or spiritual. The main point is that a man's behavior, including his thought life, represents his attempt to deal successfully with those needs which demand satisfaction and create tension within him. When they are not satisfied the person becomes frustrated and tense and spontaneously develops thoughts and/or engages in behavior designed to satisfy these needs and relieve the tension and frustration. A person chronically frustrated and tense from too many unsatisfied needs tends to feel anxious, dissatisfied and unhappy. As the tension and frustration accumulate, he tries more drastic methods in an attempt to relieve the situation.

Behavior which tends to satisfy these needs and thus reduce the inward tension, which does not harm the person himself or others, and which is morally and socially acceptable, is normal and healthy. But behavior which inadequately satisfies these needs, which fails to effectively reduce the inward tension, which is harmful either to the person himself or to others, and which is morally or socially unacceptable, is abnormal and unhealthy.

These human needs are not evil and are never designated as evil by the Bible. (Remember that the proper goal for satisfaction of all needs, physical, psychological, or spiritual, is that the Christian may be a fit vessel for serving God.) The resulting thoughts and behavior, directed toward the satisfaction of these needs, may be either good or evil, depending on what methods are used.

A man has a physical need to eat food and drink water which creates a tension building up to hunger and thirst. To satisfy these needs he develops a conscious desire to obtain food and water. Up to this point nothing evil has taken place. Now he can direct his behavior toward working at some useful occupation to earn some money and then buy food and drink. Or he can grow some crops on his farm or in his garden and get water from the lake or some other water source. So far these methods are good. But if he decides to steal someone else's food and drink, then this is evil. Although satisfying some of his needs, he frustrates other needs (such as the need to be free of guilt and shame) and arouses the righteous anger of other people toward him. This method gets him into trouble by creating more problems. Now he has to bear not only his own guilt over stealing but also a fear of being hunted down and punished by others.

Another example is the desire for sexual intercourse. To engage in courtship, to marry a suitable partner, and to seek sexual satisfaction with one's marital partner is normal and good. But to seek a partner for sexual intercourse outside of marriage is wrong. It is not the need that is bad or unhealthy, but the method (fornication or adultery) used to satisfy the need.

The concept of conflict also enters into this theory. Frequently a person may have two or more needs, all good in themselves, which cannot be satisfied simultaneously. For example, a person wants to sleep late one morning, yet he must be at work on time in order to keep his job and thus earn a living. Since both needs cannot be satisfied, he experiences frustration and tension. The conflict is resolved by his decision that one of the needs is more important than the other and therefore has priority. If there seems to be no possible resolution of the conflict, as neither of the needs can be relinquished, then the tension continues, unabated. The mental concern over such a conflict is called "psychological anxiety." When psychological anxiety is not handled in a healthy way it gives rise to mental symptoms. This state of anxiety can be very painful. If a person is hungry, but knows that he can obtain food in a few hours, he is merely uncomfortable. But if he believes that no food is available and he will die of starvation, he will experience not only hunger, but intense psychological anxiety. Such anxiety also occurs when a person has inward desires or feelings that he believes are dangerous or wrong. Notice that it is the environment *as he perceives it to be* which a person responds to with anxiety. Sometimes a person may misinterpret or perceive incorrectly the world about him and develop anxiety needlessly. The danger may be only imagined.

Since mental symptoms are expressions of conflict and anxiety, they can be considered less effective, substitute behavior patterns which are brought into use when more normal and effective patterns seem impossible. The closer to the real thing the substitute is, the more healthy is the substitution. For example, a woman who longs to have a child but who cannot may accept a career as a first grade teacher as a substitute for her desired career as a mother. This is a healthy substitution. However, if this woman denies the reality of her situation and imagines herself pregnant, this is unhealthy.

Basic Needs That Motivate Man

There are a number of different kinds of needs which interact to produce multiple desires in a person. Here is a list of obvious needs, which is not intended to be all-inclusive.

Physiological Needs

We have biological needs because we are live human beings who must maintain physical well-being. We recognize two kinds of instinctual drives in this area: libidinal and aggressive.

Libidinal. This term is not synonymous with the desire for sexual intercourse, but is broader in scope. It includes this as well as the desire to seek pleasurable sensations in any form. We derive pleasure from eating, from a hot bath, from sexual relations, from a body massage, or from the feel of comfortable clothes on our skin; in short, from anything that creates a pleasurable sensation.

Aggressive. These impulses are related to our safety and physical well-being. It is normal to desire to keep healthy. The desire to keep alive with food (satisfy hunger) is a good example of this. Notice the difference between appetite, referring to the pleasurable sensations of eating good food (libidinal pleasure), and hunger, referring to the aggressive tendency of a person to eat in order to sustain life (satisfaction of aggression). The wish to preserve one's life, to eat food, to get sufficient sleep, rest, and relaxation, to guard against injury, to keep warm in cold weather or cool in hot weather, and to pursue goals in life, are all expressions of aggression. In actual experience, of course, our actions stem from a mixture of both libidinal and aggressive needs. For example, eating is a mixture of pleasure and necessity. We have to eat to remain alive, but eating may also be pleasurable.

Individual Psychological Needs

This group of needs originates within the person himself and does not necessarily involve any contact with others. I will discuss the basic psychological needs of the average adult human being, understanding that infants and elders have essentially the same needs with minor variations.

Psychological comfort. A person experiencing tension because of a frustrated need or conflict, should attempt to either resolve the conflict, or give outward expression to the tension, or both. This process of controlling one's reactions within an optimal range to gain psychological comfort is called homeostasis. For example, a person made tense by prolonged isolation from other people would need companionship to relieve his feelings of loneliness.

Psychological satisfaction. A man with a desire for sexual intercourse would need to approach his wife and seek sexual relations. If he had no wife, and if he lacked moral convictions about fornication, he might seek some available woman as a sexual partner. If he had moral convictions, he might remain sexually frustrated. Or if he were blocked from having an available woman, he might turn to masturbation. If he had a psychological block against normal heterosexual relationships, he might turn to a deviate form of sexual behavior, such as homosexuality. Or he might stifle and repress his sexual urges and redirect their energy toward a nonsexual goal, such as art, music, athletics or some other skilled activity. If he could do none of the above, he might be forced to repress his sexual urges and permit them expression only in disguised form as mental symptoms.

A child whose important needs were frustrated in childhood may continue to seek satisfaction for these needs in adult life, engaging in behavior inappropriate to an adult situation. A son who lacked a good mother may look for someone to mother him when he is an adult, seeking delayed satisfaction and expression of his needs.

Psychological security. A man who does not want to lose his job needs to do his work well in order to avoid criticism from his boss. A man who wants his wife to love and appreciate him tries to notice and satisfy his wife's needs. A man who wants to be liked and accepted develops a need to avoid contact with people who act unfriendly and rejecting. A man who wants to preserve his life develops a need to either avoid someone who threatens his life or to attack and render ineffective that threatening person.

People frequently develop habits with the goal of avoiding situations which create anxiety. For example, an insecure person may avoid making public speeches. The psychoanalytic theory recognizes at least five basic causes of anxiety. They are fear of: (1) loss of a love object, (2) loss of love for the love object,

(3) guilt and the accompanying punishment, (4) being damaged or hurt (castration anxiety), and (5) death. I would add a sixth: (6) the fear of spending eternity in hell after death. Any situation in life, real or imagined, which threatens to or does arouse any of these fears can cause great anxiety. Relief of this anxiety is necessary if one is to maintain a feeling of security.

Need for expression. Strong emotions always seek some form of expression. They are partially expressed, automatically, through our body. For instance, the man who is afraid may sweat, his mouth may become dry, his heart may start racing, and his blood pressure may rise, augmenting his conscious feelings of fear. In addition to these automatic outlets, the energy of the strong emotion seeks an outlet in some type of motor behavior, involving action. It may only be the action of talking it over with a friend and expressing the feelings in conversation. This may give adequate expression to the emotion and allow the tension to subside. People who cannot give adequate outward expression to strong emotions (who bottle up emotions) may develop psychosomatic diseases, such as a stomach ulcer, diarrhea, high blood pressure, or mental symptoms.

One patient had experienced grief when she was a young child, at the loss of her father. She had never adequately expressed the many emotions of grief and fear that were aroused at that time. She had been discouraged from crying and had had no one she could freely talk to about the problem. So instead of expressing these feelings she repressed them. In adult life, years later, these emotions were still seeking release. They were finally expressed during a psychotherapy session with her psychiatrist, after which she felt better (more comfortable psychologically).

Another patient had been badly mistreated throughout her childhood by her mother. This aroused anger in the girl, but the mother had held her in fear of her life, permitting her no expression of anger and no self-assertion. In adult life, while undergoing psychotherapy, this woman finally expressed her strong feelings of anger toward her mother by talking them out with her psychiatrist. It took her a year to give adequate expression to these emotions which she had repressed many years before.

When emotions are not adequately expressed, they tend to appear in the substitute form of mental symptoms. One who represses anger may develop the symptom of depression, or he may become irritable, emotionally upset, or overactive. He may resort to living in a dream world or may develop any neurotic or psychotic symptom. Strong emotions need to be expressed in a psychologically healthy and socially acceptable way to insure mental health.

Need for self-control to avoid destructive behavior. Everyone recognizes the need for some self-control. One of the things a child lacks and longs for is control over his feelings and impulses. During early childhood the child must depend on his parents to help maintain this control. Normally as he grows up, he gradually develops his own set of controls. A person who lacks sufficient control over himself feels anxious at times, fearing what he may do.

The fear of one's impulses is logically related to the danger of doing something that will bring harm to oneself or to others. One cannot mistreat a friend, for very long at least, without running the risk of losing the friendship. One cannot physically attack someone without running the risk of being hurt in retaliation. The need for some degree of self-control is always present.

Need to avoid pain. A person may do something wrong and then feel so ashamed and guilty that he represses the act and the associated guilt, and "forgets" it. By repression I refer to the process by which one pushes a thought or feeling down deep into the mind where there is little or no conscious awareness of it. Although still subconsciously present, it is "forgotten," in order to avoid the point of feeling it on a conscious level. A person who represses guilt is resorting to a drastic and unhealthy method. Consciously controlled expression of the feeling in some acceptable way is a much preferred outlet. Yet it is true that all of us use some repression. A child represses many childhood emotional problems. Often painful memories are repressed and thus forgotten. This is healthy, up to a point. It is the repression of too many unresolved conflicts or of too strong emotions that is unhealthy.

Repression is considered the basic mechanism for dealing with undesired thoughts or feelings, but there are other mechanisms used to reinforce repression such as: sublimation; denial; projection; introjection; reaction formation; undoing; isolation; regression; reversal; turning against the self; and identification. These are all special psychological terms which refer to mental maneuvers. Their definitions can be found in a psychiatric dictionary. They are called "defense mechanisms" since they help the person defend himself against a conscious awareness of the thought or feeling which is disliked.

Avoidance or misperception of reality. For example, a person who is extremely sensitive to criticism may consistently fail to "notice" his own mistakes, yet be acutely aware of the mistakes of others. Or a man afraid of women may not be aware that a woman is flirting with him. For if he acknowledged it he would have to cope with his fear of women, which would make him anxious. Another example is the mother who is extremely sensitive to any criticism of herself as a mother. Because a bad child might suggest a poor mother, she is unable to perceive any faults in her children. Others can see them, but she cannot. An extreme example is the person who loses a loved one in death but is unable to accept the reality of the loss and denies that the death has occurred. Such behavior is psychotic.

We all tend to see things the way we want and need to see them. It is a sign of emotional maturity to be able to push aside this tendency and see things objectively.

Need for identity. Everyone enters the world without a formed personality, but as one matures he develops a personality—becomes a certain type of person. In order to do this he must accept as his own the ethical values and principles of some group of people. The first people to leave impressions on the developing child are parents, brothers, and sisters. Next in importance are friends from the neighborhood, school, church, and other groups. From these many sources the person selects those qualities that he likes in others and adopts them. If he admires honesty, he identifies with those who are honest, tending to model himself after them. If he fails to identify sufficiently with anyone, he ends up lacking an identity. This results in a very confused person who does not know how to act because he does not know who or what he is.

A person who lacks identity often feels empty and depressed. He usually has trouble getting along with others. Because he lacks a definite personality he is unstable in his relationships. He may act one way today and a different way tomorrow. He likes something one day, but tomorrow he has lost interest.

Need for self-esteem. Each person needs to examine himself, measuring his performance with the desired standard and deciding whether he is achieving an adequate level of performance. Since we want to think of ourselves as having admirable qualities, criticism tends to lower our self-esteem and evoke a response in us. The most healthy response to just criticism is an attempt to improve. Some people react defensively and try to explain away the criticism, thus attempting to maintain their self-esteem. Of course when the criticism is unjust and inaccurate, defense is normal.

The person who has qualities or tendencies which he recognizes as bad (through self-criticism) will tend to lack self-esteem, and is often said to have an "inferiority complex." We tend to avoid people and situations that produce the effect of lowering our self-esteem, and are drawn to those who build us up. A husband and wife should help each other maintain their self-esteem by giving each other a certain amount of encouragement.

INTERPERSONAL PSYCHOLOGICAL (SOCIAL) NEEDS

This group of psychological needs is composed of satisfactions we cannot achieve by ourselves, but only by interaction with other people. Some people avoid contact with others in real life, yet their need of people is brought out in their fantasy life. They daydream about the type of relationships they would like to have, but lack in reality.

Need to be loved. This need is obvious, although some people try to deny its existence. The person who is unloved or feels unloved is usually unhappy. One of the most harmful experiences a person can have is living in a home where he is not loved or is rejected by those he lives with. When one or both partners do not love the other it is very hard to make a marriage work.

A common cause of deep anxiety is the fear of losing someone's love or of losing the person himself. The most obvious example of this is the normal depressive reaction (mourning) following a loved one's death. This need to be loved is very strong and motivates much of our behavior.

Need for someone to love. Besides needing to be loved, every person needs an object of love. The wife needs a husband she can love, as well as a husband who will love her. A child needs to feel that he has someone to love, as do adults.

Before we invest our love in another person, we want to feel that it is safe to do so. For instance, it is painful to offer one's love to someone, only to have it rejected. There must be a recognizable positive response to our love before we can feel it is accepted. A common marital problem is that of the wife who frequently tells her husband she loves him and offers him affection, yet he seldom reciprocates and tells her he also loves her. A wife in this position begins to feel that her husband is unresponsive to her love.

This need for love is so great that sometimes people distort the reality of an ordinary human relationship and pretend it is a love relationship. Some women, for instance, have affairs with several different men, pretending they are in love with each one, when such love actually does not exist.

Need to be accepted. This is different from the need to be loved, although somewhat related. A man does not expect his boss to love him, but he wants to feel that he is liked and accepted by the boss. He wants to feel that the boss approves of his work.

A wife and husband want to feel that they are liked by each other and have each other's approval. Likewise, a child wants to feel that he has the approval of his parents, and later of his playmates and friends.

Sometimes the person whose approval is sought is hard to please and overly critical of himself and others; he may be a perfectionist. To try to win the approval of a perfectionist is usually a hopeless goal and should be abandoned. The perfectionist always manages to criticize even a good performance.

A problem is always created when a group of people refuse to accept a newcomer. When this is due to the newcomer's failure to act friendly, then a change in behavior on his part may bring acceptance, or it may not. Some groups of people are snobbish and reject others for unjustifiable reasons, and it always hurts to feel rejected.

Need for emotional support. This need is often called "dependency." It is the need to lean on others or to receive reassurance from others. The growing child needs much reassurance as he may become upset by many things. He needs to be able to go to his parents and receive help and reassurance. The child who gets too little support as a child ends up feeling insecure as an adult and may continue to be dependent. However, it is normal at a time of crisis, for a person to turn to a doctor or pastor or close friend to receive emotional encouragement and support.

Need for companionship. Everyone needs some contact with other human beings, if only in a superficial and distant way. Some people have even become temporarily mentally ill due partly to prolonged isolation from other people.

Aside from the fact that we need people for specific purposes (such as love, etc.) we also need people for companionship. For example, to watch a ball game alone is not at all the same as if others are present in the audience. We need to share things with others, to do things together.

Need for personality development. We need to develop behavior habits which give us the feeling of being a person and which help us gain from others satisfaction of our needs. This need is closely related to the need for an identity mentioned previously. What we are to ourselves constitutes our identity. What we are to others (how we affect them, etc.) constitutes our personality. I have often heard people say, "I wish I had a good personality." What they mean is they wish they had a set of behavior patterns which would evoke the desired response in others and bring satisfaction of their needs.

Need to be recognized as a person, with the rights of an individual. This need is often frustrated in an unhappy marriage where one or both of the partners refuses to acknowledge the presence and importance of the thoughts and feelings of his mate. Such a person might think of his marital partner only as a source of satisfaction to himself. He might think of his partner only as a thing to be used. This is a failure to recognize that the partner is also a person with needs and thoughts and feelings.

Need for appreciation. We all need to feel that we are doing something worthwhile. A doctor may enjoy his work because he is relieving the suffering of others. A wife may feel she is doing something worthwhile in learning to be a good cook and providing good meals for her family. However, that wife needs and should get some recognition of her accomplishment as a cook. Her family should compliment her on her cooking. To want such praise is not pride but merely a normal human need. However, the person who wants excessive praise may be neurotic.

Religious Psychological (Spiritual) Needs

Our spiritual needs are related to our attitude about God and our relationship with Him. An awareness of moral concepts and the need to satisfactorily deal with them is present in everyone. Although a person may repress and deny them, they still exist, and guilt develops when they are violated.

Need to recognize the existence of God and consciously deal with this fact. In every human being there is an awareness, conscious or subconscious, of the existence of God. The only exception to this may be the person who is a mental defective. Psalm 14:1 says that a fool may say in his heart, "There is no God." The word "fool" refers to people who lack common sense. A person whose brain is damaged may not be able to put together the facts and grasp the concept that there is a God.

The Bible makes a valid claim that the obvious orderly arrangement of the universe offers sufficient proof that it was created by an intelligent Being (Ps. 19:2). "For the invisible things of Him since the creation of the world are clearly seen, inasmuch as they are perceived by the things that are made, [such invisible things as] both His eternal inherent power and [His] divinity, so that they are inexcusable [when they reject this obvious fact]" (expanded, literal translation of Romans 1:20). To say that the universe could have happened by chance is a ridiculous assertion and is contrary to the obvious fact that things do not arrange themselves in an orderly way by chance.

How does one explain, then, how some intelligent people today can consciously believe and say, "There is no God"? The explanation is that they have repressed deeply into their subconscious mind their awareness of God's existence. Although they may consciously deny it, deep in their hearts they know that God does exist.

Why do they hide from this knowledge? Because it disturbs them, and we all tend to avoid things which upset us. The acceptance of the existence of God leads to the thought that this God, our Creator, is more powerful than we are, and that He must be reckoned with some day. The thought of this fills men with anxiety, unless they know that their relationship with God is safe and secure.

The history of mankind offers evidence of this need. Men everywhere, knowing that there is a God, have tried to worship him, often incorrectly. Men tend to think of God the way they want to picture Him, and end up worshiping a god who does not exist. For instance, there is no such thing as a god who wants to be worshiped by the senseless burning alive of human sacrifices. Yet some people have thought of God in this way. Paul rebuked the Greeks for thinking of God incorrectly (Acts 17:29).

Everyone must deal in some way with his own awareness of God. To repress this knowledge into the subconscious mind does not settle the problem. It persists there as a source of disturbing feelings that prevent contentment and inner peace.

Need to establish peaceful contact with God. Men have a need to "get right with God." This need is clearly illustrated by the man who approached Christ asking about eternal life (Matt. 19:16). Although this man had tried from his youth to obey all the commandments, he was aware that he still lacked something (v. 20). He had not established contact with God, and therefore he felt unsure about his life in eternity. Instead of worshiping God, he worshiped money (vv. 22-24). Christ advised him to give up his false god (money), and to come to the true God (Christ the Son of God). When the man did not do this he went away disturbed (grieved, v. 22).

A man may have many material possessions, good physical and mental health, and many obvious sources of happiness. Yet his soul will never quite be at rest until he has made his peace with God. Paul the apostle said, "godliness associated with contentment is great gain" (literal translation of I Tim. 6:6). Godliness refers to having the right attitude toward God and the habit of behaving properly toward God. Contentment is the word *autarkeia* which, literally, is "soul-sufficiency." It suggests the idea of having the needs of one's soul satisfied sufficiently. But this peaceful contentment of the soul is linked to the concept of godliness—having a right relationship to God. "There is no peace, saith the LORD, unto the wicked" (Isa. 48:22). "But the wicked are like the troubled sea, when it cannot rest, whose waters cast up mire and dirt" (Isa. 57:20). How do we achieve peace with God?

Peace is the great message of the gospel of the Lord Jesus Christ. Peter referred to this message as "preaching peace through Jesus Christ" (Acts 10:36). Paul said that now we (Christians) have peace with God through our Lord Jesus Christ, and linked this peace to the fact of our being pronounced righteous by faith (Rom. 5:1). How can this transaction be accomplished?

One must first accept the fact that every human being has, in some way, sinned and fallen short of the standard of holiness required by God for entrance into heaven and into God's presence (Rom. 3:23). No one is righteous, standing on his own record (Ps. 14:1-3; Rom. 3:10-12). No one who is not pronounced righteous and cleansed from sin will ever stand in the presence of God in a good peaceful relationship (Hab. 1:13), for God hates sin and sinners (Ps. 5:4-5). The alienation between God and man is caused by man's sin (Col. 1:21).

The way that God has designated to remedy this alienation is by removing the barrier of sin. We are reckoned righteous in the eyes of God by the free gift of forgiveness which God offers us, based on the fact that Christ, the Son of God, has died for our sins (Matt. 20:28; Rom. 5:6, 8; I Cor. 15:3; I Thess. 5:9-10). Paul makes it clear that it is a free gift, which cannot be earned by human effort, in Ephesians 2:8-9. This righteousness is available through the acceptance of Christ as one's personal Saviour on the principle of faith (Acts 10:43; Rom. 1:16-17; 3:22, 28; 4:5; Eph. 2:8).

God can forgive our sins on the basis that Christ has paid the penalty for them. Our guilt was reckoned to Christ, so that His righteousness might be reckoned to us (II Cor. 5:21). We are cleansed from our sins by the blood (that is, the death) of Christ (Rev. 1:5). After being cleansed, we can enjoy peace with God (Rom. 5:1; Col. 1:20).

The need for salvation is a basic need of everyone. The lack of it will always produce some discontent within the soul. This lack of peace within the soul is easily seen in a dying man who has never made his peace with God. His anxiety is understandable since he is leaving this life unprepared for the next life in which he will have to stand before God and be judged.

At this point I want to restate an important principle. Some Christians think that just becoming a Christian will solve any psychological problem. This is not true. Becoming a Christian will relieve only that psychological anxiety which was related to the unsaved condition. For example, a person worrying about what he might experience in hell could stop worrying, knowing that he was going to heaven. Psychological problems not stemming from the unsaved condition would have to be solved by the remedy specifically suited to each particular problem. For example, a person who feels that no human being could love him would still tend to feel unlovable, in spite of the fact that God loves him.

Need to maintain a good relationship with God. A non-Christian has a need to get right with God. The Christian has a need to stay right with Him. A Christian also has a desire to stay on good terms with God, just as a son wants to stay in good relationship with his father. This involves many things, but it can be summed up by the goal of: living a life pleasing to God. (This point is developed further in chapter 8.)

Need to seek security and blessing in the present life. The previously discussed need had to do with our relationship to God both now and for eternity. But we also have a need for God's blessings in this life, such as: good health, prosperity, happiness, safety, and other desirable things. Men have always—sometimes ignorantly, incorrectly, and selfishly—sought the blessing of God on their life. In the past, men ignorantly conceived of a god of the ground and prayed to him, asking for blessings on their crops. Such a god, of course, did not exist.

When men are in great danger or distress, it is common for them to turn to God and beg His help or blessing. Yet these same men may have never tried to establish contact with God before. They either do not realize or will not face the fact that God does not ordinarily hearken to the prayers of any but the righteous (that is, true Christians) (I Peter 3:12).

Peter, in his appeal to Christians to live a godly life, indicates that God blesses the lives of those who turn away from evil and seek that which is good (I Peter 3:10-12). To live a life oriented toward the practice of evil is to frustrate this need for God's blessing and suffer dissatisfaction.

Avoidance of guilt. Everyone has the need to avoid feelings of guilt, for guilt tends to depress a person, lowering his self-esteem and confidence. To do that which is evil is costly, and one of the prices which must be paid is the burden of guilt and loss of self-esteem. The actual experience of feeling guilty is very unpleasant. Sometimes people can repress into the subconscious mind both the memory of the guilty act and the guilty feeling associated with it. But this does not work very well, because there it continues to bother them, producing emotional discomfort. They may not consciously feel guilty, but inwardly they are guilty and disturbed.

Peter mentioned fleshly lusts which, by producing sin (James 1:15), and thus guilt, war against the soul (I Peter 2:11). Paul warned that "he who sows to the flesh [that is, the sin nature or tendency] shall reap corruption from the flesh" (Gal. 6:8).

It is clear from Romans 2:15 that everyone has the law written in his heart. By this Paul meant a moral law—the awareness of right and wrong. (Of course, this can be diminished by brain damage or confused by insanity.) The conscience is there, to tell us when we are morally wrong and to make us feel guilty whenever we violate one of God's eternal moral laws. These moral laws are mentioned in Exodus 20 and Matthew 19. They might be summarized as follows: (1) Worship and love the true God and none other (Exodus 20:3-5). (2) Do not use the name of God profanely (Exodus 20:7). (3) Do not commit murder (Exodus 20:13; Matt. 19:18). (4) Do not commit fornication or incest or adultery or any sexually deviate act (such as bestiality or homosexuality) (Exodus 20:14; Matt. 19:18). (5) Do not steal (Exodus 20:15; Matt. 19:18). (6) Do not lie (that is, bear false witness) (Exodus 20:16; Matt. 19:18). (7) Show proper respect and treatment toward your parents (Exodus 20:12; Matt. 19:19) (8) Do not covet (that is, lust: a desire so unreasonably strong it tends to carry one into sins such as murder, robbery, adultery, etc.) (Exodus 20:17; Rom. 7:7). (9) Love your neighbor as yourself (Lev. 19:18; Matt. 19:19). An act is wrong if it violates one or more of these laws.

To clarify the issue, anyone breaking one of these laws, no matter what culture he is living in, would feel guilty. One who commits murder feels some guilt, even if murder is commonplace in his society. Cultural tendencies and customs can affect the degree of guilt, sometimes making it more or less intense.

The need to avoid guilt gives rise to a desire to do that which is right. However, this desire to do the right thing is opposed by another tendency in man to do that which is wrong, especially under stress. Under stress, men may become quite evil. So, the feeling of guilt is painful and there is a need to avoid it.

Need to atone for guilt. When one has done something wrong and experiences guilt, he feels a need to atone, to make up in some way for the wrong act. Sometimes he deliberately does something good, hoping to cancel out the wrong deed. If he hurts someone unjustly, he might try to do the person a favor to make up for it.

The hardened gangster, made rich by his plunder, may make generous donations to worthy organizations, as if to atone for his crimes. It is also common for someone who has performed a criminal act to give himself up, for the purpose of taking his punishment and easing his sense of guilt. We sometimes try to punish ourselves for things about which we feel guilty. Frequently there is a self-punitive element associated with mental symptoms. In some ways this need produces good results. It helps us to get over our unjust resentment of others and act friendlier toward them. As far as our salvation is concerned, we cannot atone for our sins. Christ paid the penalty for them and when we put our trust in Him, the guilt for our sins is settled once and for all (Heb. 9:28; 10:10, 12, 14).

ABNORMAL PSYCHOLOGICAL NEEDS

All of the needs mentioned previously are normal and are found in everyone. However, it is possible to develop abnormal psychological needs. These may be exaggerations of normal needs or they may be peculiar, pathological needs which are the result of warped attempts to satisfy more basic needs.

One example is the person who seems to have an insatiable desire for attention from others. The need is abnormal because of its great intensity. Such a person may do anything just to get attention.

Another example is a need which is normal in childhood but which is inappropriate in adult situations, and therefore abnormal. For instance, a need to receive parental-type love is normal for a child but not for an adult. The adult who seeks someone to cater to his needs and treat him indulgently as a parent would treat a child is abnormal.

Another example is the person who is sadistic, that is, who has a need to hurt others. At some earlier time in his life he may have been attacked and had reason to fight back. But only his original attacker deserves punishment, not everyone else, and a sadistic person seeks to hurt everyone.

Such abnormal needs are difficult to overcome without the help of a psychiatrist, although the patient himself may be distressed by the need and wish to eliminate it.

INTERPLAY OF NEEDS (HOMEOSTASIS)

Gratification vs. Frustration. It is obvious that one cannot have everything he wants in this life, but it is healthy aggression to aim for it. It is wrong not to have any goals, for this is certain to lead to frustration. As our needs press for satisfaction, we can respond in different ways, but complete relief from the tension never occurs. In this life there will always be longing for basic needs and motivation toward one or more goals. For example, the man who wants to avoid starvation must work and earn money to buy food. He becomes tense if he cannot work due to illness, an accident, or loss of a job. These events tend to upset his balance temporarily. The normal result is an increased level of tension which allows him enough energy for productive activity, but does not cause him to suffer emotionally or become mentally ineffective. It is evident that unusually productive men are frequently very tense people. The process of maintaining the proper level of tension is called homeostasis.

When tension (from unsatisfied needs or psychological conflicts) builds up, there are several ways of responding to it:

Healthy responses. These are planned, logical actions which are meant to satisfy the needs or resolve the conflict, without producing more problems. Healthy responses may also include hostile, aggressive, or flight reactions which are appropriate to the situation. Sometimes it is best to fight, sometimes better to flee, even if it means giving up hope of satisfying the wish. One must choose the course of action appropriate to the situation.

Vindicative fight responses. These are hostile, aggressive actions which are not appropriate to the situation, but only serve to strike back at that which seems to be causing the person pain. They are not healthy and not only are ineffective in resolving the problem, but serve to create additional problems.

Examples of this type of response are irritability, belligerence, and open unjust hostility. If these fight responses are repressed into the subconscious mind, the person might develop almost any neurotic, psychotic, or psychosomatic symptoms. But if these feelings are openly expressed toward innocent people, they may provoke resentment.

Panicky flight responses. These actions represent an attempt to flee from that which seems to be causing the pain. They are not healthy because they are inappropriate and ineffective. Common examples are blind running away, malingering, and laziness. A severe form is regression to childish behavior patterns, which is evident in some forms of schizophrenia. Another example is the person who gives up the attempt to live a responsible, adult life and tries to manipulate others into caring for him because he is "sick."

Combination of fight and flight responses. A mixture of fight and flight behavior also occurs. All of these responses to tension and conflict produce associated physical responses in the body called emotional reactions. Properly speaking, an emotional reaction is a psychological response which is accompanied by some bodily sensation, such as pounding of the heart, upset stomach, or a headache. All of these sensations are caused by the overflow of tension as it seeks expression through the body. Most psychological responses produce some bodily sensations or emotions.

HIERARCHY OF NEEDS

Our behavior is always the result of an inner compromise regarding our needs. Our various needs compete with one another for gratification, and the needs most pressing at the moment are given priority. As a general rule, needs for safety and security take precedence over all others. The average person in a dangerous situation will think first about the need to save his life. But if he deeply loves someone else who is in danger he may put that person's safety above his own.

One of the benefits of being a Christian is that if we are cooperative with the Spirit of God, we can be trained by God to put spiritual needs above natural human needs. Some Christians are willing even to die if necessary, to bring honor and glory to God. The Holy Spirit competes with our human nature in our decision as to which needs will receive priority (Gal. 5:17). Only the Christian can develop within himself the need to have a goal higher than his own good. To be healthy and happy for the sake of oneself is good, but such a goal is even better if it has the ultimate purpose of being fit for service to God and others.

We should evaluate our needs to see which we give priority to. The Christian who gives priority to spiritual needs will become a more spiritual person. The giving of priority is an act of the intellect, a conscious decision. A mind too disrupted by mental conflict and tension is not able to make a wise decision and thus tends to give more priority to those needs involved in the conflict. For this reason spiritual needs tend to be pushed aside until the painful tension is relieved.

A word of caution is necessary. It is a mistake to completely ignore spiritual needs and be preoccupied with ordinary human needs. But it is also a mistake to become too preoccupied with spiritual needs and neglect normal temporal needs, thus living an unbalanced life. No one can escape completely from the basic needs of food, rest, relaxation, and recreation. To what extent should dedicated Christians gratify these needs? Enough to stay healthy and happy without being addicted to the mad pursuit of pleasure. This is one reason some Christians become mentally disturbed. They recognize God's spiritual laws, but fail to conform to His physical and psychological laws. In seeking to be more spiritual they attempt to live an unnatural life, as though they were no longer bound by natural laws.

It is important to determine what needs should be put first. The man who approached Christ, seeking eternal life, was instructed to stop worshiping money as a god and turn to Christ for eternal life (Matt. 19:20-21). But to free himself from the false god of money he would have had to get rid of his wealth and endure the frustration of not gratifying many needs and wants which he was accustomed to satisfying. He put these material and physical needs first and relegated his need for eternal life to a less important position. Although he had been dissatisfied before talking to Christ, after rejecting Christ he was "sorrowful" (v. 22). He knew exactly what was wrong: he lacked eternal life and was addicted to worshiping a false god, money. His downgrading of spiritual needs cost him peace of soul in his present life, in addition to depriving him of eternal life with God. Likewise the Christian needs to give careful thought to the priority he gives to spiritual needs.

Psychologically Traumatic Events

Just as a physical accident or illness upsets the body physiologically, certain events may upset a person psychologically. Some such events are: death of a loved one; divorce; rejection of love or friendship; sadistic treatment, either physically or psychologically; loss of a job; loss of health; loss of eyesight or hearing; or loss of an arm or leg. Everyone would react psychologically to one of these things. These events temporarily upset the psychological balance and require a readjustment to cope with the accompanying frustration and tension.

Seemingly good events can sometimes be very upsetting. For example, a man who does not want any more responsibility in his job but who is promoted to a responsible position anyway may become quite tense. He may respond by developing a stomach ulcer. The birth of an unplanned and unwanted baby may produce great disappointment and dissatisfaction and create financial and psychological problems. Failure to achieve a goal may also cause psychological distress. For example, a college student may flunk a final exam.

All of these events are psychologically traumatic and cause stress in the adult. The child is even more vulnerable and easily damaged. For example, a child who is rejected by his parents or does not feel loved by them may despair and conclude that no one will ever love him. As he grows up feeling unlovable, he may fear rejection. He may withdraw from people to avoid being hurt again, as he was hurt by his parents. By the time he is an adult, he may be a "loner." We have to face the reality that it is possible for a child to be damaged so severely in childhood that he grows up to be a psychological invalid. Too many hurts leave too many scars in both the physical and psychological realms.

To summarize, we tend to behave in a manner that we think will bring relief from pain and gratification of our needs as we perceive them.

Classification of Mental Disorders

A mental disorder may develop either as the end result of an attempt to cope with problems stemming from a poor childhood environment, from a severe crisis occurring in adult life, or from a combination of the two. Regardless of the cause, the types of mental disorders can be divided into several different groups as follows:

ORGANIC BRAIN SYNDROMES

These have already been discussed in chapter 6 under physical causes. They are mental disorders stemming primarily from organic (physical) diseases of the body which affect brain function.

FUNCTIONAL DISORDERS

These are primarily due to psychological problems involving frustration or conflict of the basic psychological needs which I have discussed earlier. People are bothered by essentially the same kinds of problems. How they try to cope with their problems determines whether they develop a character disorder, a neurotic disorder, a psychosomatic disorder, or a psychosis. Usually a patient suffers from a mixture of these, with one type predominating.

Character disorders or behavior disorders. The psychological problem is expressed by an action which is an attempt (usually partly or wholly unsuccessful) to resolve or escape from the problem. The behavior may temporarily relieve the tension. But because the problem itself is not solved, the tension reaccumulates and thus the behavior recurs.

The behavior may be objectionable to the person himself, to others, or to both. For example, the person who has a homosexual character disorder may be quite dissatisfied with this aspect of himself. On the other hand, a compulsive thief may arouse more anger in others than in himself. A person with a character disorder, although subconsciously very anxious, frequently manages to feel consciously comfortable as long as he continues to behave in that characteristic way which relieves his tension.

One example of a character disorder which society does not usually object to is the compulsive worker. Such a man may work hard and unusually long hours at the office and then have to keep busy working at home to avoid becoming disturbed. He has to keep working and cannot take time to relax.

To summarize, this way of coping with problems involves using behavior as an outlet for the tension and as an attempt to resolve the problem. The behavior becomes a habit and thus becomes part of one's character or personality.

Psychosomatic disorders. The body is a main outlet for expression of the problems and associated tension. One may break out in a skin rash when he gets upset. Another may develop asthma or stomach trouble. The association between emotions and duodenal ulcers is well known. This method is universal. Whenever a person has any great emotional upset, his body is affected. The average person may become nauseated or develop a headache. But when the psychological problems are deep and the person resorts to this method of coping with them, he may develop a disease that lasts as long as he continues to have his problems. Since the problems continue to generate tension, the disease process continues.

Neurotic disorders. The neurotic patient may develop a feeling of extreme anxiety, an illogical fear (phobia), a senseless compulsive activity (such as repeated hand washing), a depressed feeling, or a dissociative reaction (such as amnesia).

The neurotic cannot successfully cope with his problems either by behavior or by expression through his body. So he has to resort to more drastic measures. The symptoms, although painful, may prevent the person from becoming aware of the problem itself which he (subconsciously) considers dreadful or dangerous. In reality, the problem usually is not as bad as he thinks.

Psychotic disorders. This is the most drastic and desperate way to cope with problems. In these cases the anxiety is so overwhelming that the person resorts to a severe distortion of reality. When the life situation as perceived by the patient seems unbearable he may deny the truth and develop a delusion. He may consciously convince himself that the problem is gone, as if by magic. Such a person retreats from the realities of life into a world of make-believe where situations are to his liking.

In this retreat he frequently loses his sense of responsibility. He may undergo an abrupt and profound personality change— he may lose his adult ways and act childlike. This is called regression. Another example of a psychotic is the person who feels unloved but develops the delusion that he is loved by everyone in the world and is uniquely superior to others.

Many so-called nervous breakdowns are actually psychotic disorders. The most common type is schizophrenia, which involves the use of denial of reality and the adoption of delusions in trying to cope with problems.

CHAPTER EIGHT

PSYCHOLOGICAL CONCEPTS AND BIBLICAL CORRELATIONS

Mental Disorders

THERE ARE A NUMBER of words in the Bible referring to mild and severe mental disorders. In Luke 10:41 Christ told Martha she was worried (inwardly anxious) and agitated (outwardly troubled and upset). In Mark 3:21 and II Corinthians 5:13 we have the word *existēmi* which means "to be beside oneself," "to be out of one's mind," "to be crazy." Mark 3:21 gives evidence that people had so little understanding of the truths that Christ preached that they thought He was insane. In Acts 26:24 and I Corinthians 14:23 we have the word *mainomai* which means "to be eager," "to be mad," "to be crazy."

People have developed mental disorders, including insanity, for thousands of years. When and how did mental disease enter the human race? The Bible gives the answer in Romans, chapter 1. Susceptibility to mental disorders came as a judgment upon men for their failure to worship God properly. Men failed to give God the glory He deserved and stupidly gave it to creatures which God had created. Because of this failure God executed judgment. He gave the human race up to a susceptibility to two things. (See the phrase "God delivered them up," used in Romans 1:24 and 1:28.) The two things are sexual perversion and mental disorders. Sexual perversion is described in Romans 1:24-27, where it is illustrated by homosexuality, the most common type of sexual perversion.

A mental disorder is described in Romans 1:28-32 as a reprobate mind. The word "reprobate" in English today means "un-
principled, unfit, undesirable; one beyond hope." The specific
meaning of the Greek word used here (*adokimos*) is "disapproved
of after being tested." For example a radio, inspected and found
to be defective would be rejected. At the time of Christ this
word was used for those contestants who failed to qualify in the
athletic games because they did not meet the approved standard.

To apply this concept to the mind, God gave men up to a
susceptibility to develop a condition where the mind fails to
function properly by normal standards. Thus we all are susceptible to mental disorders. This does not mean that all will develop
a mental disorder, but that all could. Because of the sin of Adam
we became susceptible to physical disease. Because of the failure
of the human race to properly worship God we also became susceptible to mental disease.

The fact that mental disease susceptibility is a judgment by
God does not mean that a mental disease in an individual does not
develop because of psychological causes. Behind every psychological disease are psychological conflicts. It is merely our *susceptibility* to mental disorders that was God's judgment.

It is noted in Romans 1:28 that as a result of this judgment men
"practice those things that are not proper" (literal translation).
Verses 29-32 describe the wrong practices: sadistic behavior;
envy; murder; strife; rebelliousness; lack of mercy; lack of natural
affection; and others. While all of these actions are sin, they are
also symptoms of psychological disorders. So the Bible recognizes mental disease as a disorder of the whole human race, developing as a judgment from God.

Psychological Maturity

Immaturity may be defined as an area in which a person, after
reaching physical maturity and chronological adulthood, continues to think or act like a child. All children start out lacking
logic and wisdom in many areas. As they have more experiences
they try to interpret causes, and often misinterpret them. This

is normal in childhood, but in adult life it is not normal and is proof of psychological immaturity.

Normally, if his environment is good enough, the child gradually gives up childish attitudes and behavior patterns and adopts more mature ones. But if his environment is bad he may grow up still thinking in an immature way. Then in adult life he will continue to misinterpret and misunderstand and misbehave as he did in childhood. This can produce many conflicts and much inappropriate behavior in adult situations. The conflict of childish versus adult ways of thinking is mentioned in I Corinthians 13:11.

Also involved in psychological immaturity is the tendency for adults to continue seeking gratification of needs which were frustrated in childhood. A man who had a negligent or absent mother may expect his wife to treat him as a good mother would treat a child. He is still seeking a mother. This causes trouble in marriage because a wife can really be only a wife. A woman married to such a man would see him as demanding and self-centered, wanting only to be catered to and indulged, becoming petulant or angry when he does not get his way. She would be frustrated by his lack of mature interest in her welfare. This is understandable since the man's mistake is in viewing his wife as a source of maternal indulgence rather than as a wife to whom he has responsibilities. In marriage each partner must meet the normal needs of the other. A marriage is disturbed when one mate acts as a parent who is always giving and the other as a child who is always taking.

Another example of immaturity is the tendency to perceive adult situations as if they were similar to earlier undesirable childhood experiences. For example, the boy who was dominated by his mother may fear being bossed by women. He may think a woman's mere suggestion is an attempt to dominate and boss him. An improvement in maturity would require his giving up this unrealistic perception and accepting the woman's suggestion for what it really was (only a suggestion) instead of what he feared it to be (a command).

Psychological Growth

Sometimes an advance in maturity can be achieved when one spontaneously becomes consciously aware of a psychological problem that was buried in the subconscious. After the problem becomes conscious he can then deal with it and resolve it, provided he wants to. Paul recommended that Christians try to judge (literally, discern) themselves (I Cor. 11:31). This is often very hard to do alone, but can be accomplished with the help of a counselor, such as a pastor or psychiatrist. God can work through the doctor to help the Christian learn the truth about himself.

Another method used by God to produce more maturity is testing. In testing a Christian experiences a situation in which he suffers emotionally or physically. In Romans 5:3-4 Paul says that the proper attitude toward tribulations will result in more patience (literally, patient endurance) and integrity of character. James (1:2-4) urges Christians to have a positive attitude toward testing, because it produces patience and helps us become more mature. (The word "perfect" in James 1:4 means "complete" or "mature.") Peter points out that testing is necessary because it helps us become free from the enslaving habits of sin (I Peter 4:1).

Psychological suffering tends to break down the usual character habits, both good and bad. When the bad, sinful habits are weakened they are easier to remove, and can be replaced by good habits, resulting in an improvement in character and growth in maturity. Improvement can be accomplished through proper response to the test. We are to be exercised by it, as an athlete is improved by exercise and does not faint (Heb. 12:5, 11). Even though the suffering may temporarily weaken good character habits also, God can be counted on to repair the damage later. In I Peter 5:10 the word "make you perfect" means to "repair."

The Heart and the Thoughts

In Philippians 4:7 and Romans 2:15 the two terms, heart and thoughts, are used, distinguishing these two areas of the mind. In Romans 1:21 it is heart and reasonings.

The existence of the deeper, subconscious part of the mind is a well-established truth. This subconscious level is present in everyone, whether they are mentally disturbed or not. We seem to need the existence of a subconscious area in order to exist comfortably psychologically. By it we can forget many disturbing thoughts and memories. It is healthier to give adequate, safe expression to such thoughts before they are repressed into the subconscious. Then they are less likely to continue disturbing us from a subconscious level.

The Tendency to Resist the Truth

Paul noticed the tendency of men to set themselves against the truth as proclaimed by others (II Tim. 3:8) and also to deny the truth to themselves (I Cor. 3:18; Gal. 6:3, 7). When a person represses something into the subconscious mind, this may be a deliberate attempt to escape from the truth. He may be trying to avoid the disturbing feelings aroused when he thinks about the truth. By this maneuver he ceases to be consciously aware of it. He may become tense or nervous as a result, but he manages to "forget" the cause.

"Defense mechanisms" are mental maneuvers designed to keep these disturbing thoughts hidden in the subconscious. They can be studied further in any textbook of psychiatry. A common example is rationalization, which is a way of trying to deny some disturbing truth. The Bible mentions this process in Romans 2:15. The inherent moral law of God, written on a man's heart, always creates a feeling of guilt whenever that man violates any part of that law (as in an act of lying, or stealing, or murder, etc.) His conscience says to him, "you are guilty." Then he either feels conscious guilt (that is, his thoughts are "accusing"), or he represses the feelings of guilt into the subconscious and tries to avoid conscious guilt (that is, his thoughts are "excusing"; literally, "defending themselves," as in last part of verse 15). To summarize, if the conscious mind cannot face up to the guilt, it produces defensive thoughts which either excuse or deny the wrong behavior.

David testifies to the fact that God desires us to have truth in the inner self (Ps. 51:6). John also urges us to walk in the light (I John 1:7), meaning to accept and acknowledge and react appropriately to all truth which we know. This is the way of psychological and spiritual health.

Conflict

Any conflict creates frustration and tension. We are all subject to conflicts and usually resolve them in some way. For example, a man may have a strong desire to buy a luxury car, but only money enough to buy a moderately priced car. He wants two conflicting things: to buy an expensive car and to remain financially solvent. Because he cannot have both, he must resolve the conflict by giving up one of the goals. If he has character he will give up the luxury car and choose to remain financially solvent. If he is irresponsible he may go ahead and buy the car, get into financial difficulty, and perhaps lose his new car because of failure to make the payments.

Many people have conflicts involving moral issues, such as an unmarried person with a desire to have sexual intercourse who also wants to live up to a moral standard which prohibits fornication. Other conflicts do not involve moral issues, such as a poor swimmer's fear of water.

More abnormal is the misinformed person who has a mistaken idea that something is wrong when really it is not. Such a person may have an abnormally severe conscience and thus may experience needless conflicts.

Psychological conflicts, with their associated nervous symptoms, are not sinful. But failure to make a valid, effective attempt to resolve a conflict and end the suffering is sinful. Why? Conflict reduces our efficiency as instruments of God (II Cor. 4:7), because our usefulness to God is hindered by anything that disturbs our physical or psychological or spiritual health. We are obligated to keep the vessels of God as healthy and clean and pure as we can (II Cor. 7:1; I John 3:3) so that He may use us in service more effectively (Rom. 6:13, 19; 12:1). It is neither wise nor spiritual for a Christian to continue suffering nervous symptoms due to psychological conflict, refusing to accept psychiatric or pastoral counsel. This is just as illogical as a Christian developing a physical illness and refusing to let a physician treat him. He reduces his efficiency as a servant of Christ.

My proof that conflict is not sinful is the fact that Christ Himself experienced severe conflict over the Cross experience and suffered several emotional symptoms until He resolved the conflict. Yet He never sinned (John 8:46; II Cor. 5:21; Heb. 4:15; I Peter 2:22; I John 3:5). What was the conflict and how did He resolve it?

Christ, being without sin, regarded the idea of death which involved His bearing the sins of everyone (I Peter 3:18) and the associated temporary state of alienation from God the Father (Matt. 27:46) as horrible. He shrank from it as a normal reaction. But He also wanted to please and obey God the Father, who had sent Him for this very purpose (Matt. 20:28; John 18:11).

From time to time during His earthly life Christ was troubled by this conflict (John 12:27). It reached a peak in the Garden of Gethsemane the night before He died on the cross. There Christ, emotionally upset, expressed this conflict to God in prayer. His words to the Father were: "My Father, since it is possible, let this cup pass away from me at once. Nevertheless, not as I desire but as You (desire)" (literal, expanded translation of Matt. 26:39). In this one sentence are expressed the two sides of the conflict. Christ wanted to avoid the cross, but He also wanted to obey God the Father.

The gospel writers use vivid words in describing His emotional state during this conflict (the following quotations are all excerpts from literal, expanded translations): "afflicted with grief," "distressed" in Matthew 26:37; "distressed," "terrifyingly amazed" in Mark 14:33; "exceedingly sorrowful" in Matthew 26:38 and Mark 14:34; "My soul is encompassed with grief, so much so that I am close to dying" in Matthew 26:38; "having entered a state of an agonizing struggle, He kept on praying more fervently. And His sweat became like clots of blood, repeatedly falling down upon the ground" in Luke 22:44.

This phenomena mentioned by Luke of bleeding through the sweat glands of the skin has been observed several times and is recorded in medical literature.[1] It is a sign of great psychological distress and tension.

Christ did not remain in conflict and suffering. He resolved the conflict by giving up hope for one of His wishes—escaping the cross (Matt. 26:42). When His conflict was resolved, the psychological distress was ended. His nervous symptoms disappeared and He was once again at peace within His soul. Here we have a clear illustration of the proper way to resolve a psychological conflict.

Christians are not only subject to the same kind of conflicts experienced by non-Christians, but also the additional conflicts of the new nature and the old nature. The goals of the Spirit often clash with the desires of our human nature (Gal. 5:17).

Depression

In II Corinthians 1:8 the word *bareō* means "to weigh down," "to depress." In Matthew 26:37 Christ is said to be "very heavy" and here it is *adēmoneō*, which means "to be distressed," "to be troubled," "to be depressed." The effect of depression on personality and judgment is recognized by Paul in II Corinthians 2:7. Here he recommended that the Corinthian church show love to a brother being disciplined for gross sin (see I Cor. 5:1), lest he be "swallowed up with sorrow."

Psychologically, depression can develop in several different forms. The first is repressed anger. Whether the anger is reasonable or unreasonable, the person is reluctant to be consciously aware of it. So he pushes it into his subconscious, producing a peculiar psycho-physiological state called "depression." This type of depression can be easily eliminated by becoming consciously aware of the anger and giving adequate expression to it in a safe manner (such as talking it out with a friend).

A second type of depression is experienced as a result of an attempt to keep something painful buried deep in the subcon-

[1]Gould and Pyle, *Anomalies and Curiosities of Medicine* (New York: Julian Press, Inc., 1956), 388-91.

scious mind. Each time the painful thought or memory threatens to erupt into conscious awareness, great anxiety is aroused, producing depression. The person must consciously face up to the disturbing thought and master it in order to rid himself of the source of depression.

A third type of depression results when a person is threatened by a real or imagined loss of something important. A man might become depressed if he lost his job, or if his self-esteem became lowered though a wrong action. The depression which follows the death of a loved one is normal and is called mourning. However, if it lasts over six months or so, it ceases to be mourning and becomes an abnormal depression. This shows the importance of having a correct sense of values. To some the loss of money (when it is treated as a god) would cause deep depression. This is discussed further under spiritual causes of nervous tension.

A fourth type is the "schizoid" depression. The person with this disorder feels "empty." This feeling is different from other types of depression. It stems from the fact that such persons avoid close relationships with other people and are often lonely.

Another type is the "schizophrenic" depression. It occurs when a schizophrenic person's feeling of identity is impaired.

Ego Control

In I Corinthians 9:25 we have the word *egkrateuomai*, which means "to have power over self," "to exercise self-control." In Titus 1:8 the noun form of the same word is used. A clearly similar word is used in Galatians 5:23 where self-control is mentioned as one of the qualities the Holy Spirit strives to produce in us.

The meaning of self-control is clearly illustrated in I Peter 2:11 where the command is given to "keep on holding yourself back from fleshly (carnal) lusts" (literal, expanded translation). We are to consciously hold ourselves back from behavior that is wrong. In order to do this we must consciously know about our desires to do wrong things.

The biblical method of dealing with antisocial and immoral strivings is not repression into the subconscious (with resulting mental symptoms) but conscious self-control. The biblical way is the way of health.

This illustrates a point I have insisted is true, that nothing recommended to the Christian by the Bible is psychologically unsound, nor does it lead to mental illness. The Bible is innocent of causing mental disease.

Self-destructive Behavior

In I Peter 2:20 Peter points out that a Christian slave cannot lay any claim to fame as a martyr when his sufferings (beatings) occur as a result of his repeated disobedience. I have noticed that some Christians, when they suffer, immediately say "God is testing me," or "He is letting me be persecuted for the faith." Yet in reality the Christian himself, through mistakes he has made, may have provoked it all by himself. An example is the preacher who, fearing his people will dislike and reject him, acts so unfriendly and impolite to them that he provokes them into rejecting him.

Many times we do bring our troubles on ourselves. To explain away a trouble as testing from God may be a convenient way of avoiding the true cause, which could be a psychological problem or a character defect. Because facing up to this defect arouses anxiety, there is a tendency to avoid it and blame something else. Sometimes this is the reason God seems to delay sending help in a trial. He wants us to see and correct our faults before He removes the trial.

How Can Psychiatric Therapy Help?

It can help in two general ways: by psychotherapy or by drug therapy.

Psychotherapy is the term used for any procedure where the doctor and patient sit down and talk. It is not a haphazard thing but a scientific, logical procedure that is based on sound psychological principles. What benefits can be obtained from it?

First, it offers a chance to exert pressure on the person to face up to a problem he has been avoiding—to face the truth. It encourages him to deal with his problems and try to resolve them in some effective way. Sometimes psychotherapy helps the patient become consciously aware of the problem, if he has repressed it into the subconscious. Once it becomes conscious then it can be discussed and resolved. As long as it stays subconscious, it cannot be resolved.

Secondly, psychotherapy is a person-to-person relationship which usually reveals incorrect attitudes that may have developed in the patient. When these attitudes produce a disturbance in the doctor-patient relationship, as they have in other personal relationships, then they can be recognized, discussed and corrected.

A third phenomenon that can take place is that a patient may relive an upsetting experience in his past, feeling again the associated emotional reaction. The result may be a feeling of relief or release, because some repressed emotions have finally been expressed. This is called abreaction.

A similar phenomenon is ventilation, which occurs when a person expresses feelings related to a more recent upsetting experience. He "lets off steam," so to speak. This should be an important normal emotional outlet for everyone. Everyone needs a person to talk to and get things off his chest.

Another function of psychotherapy is reeducation. Many times disturbed married couples have to be reeducated as to the principles to be observed for a happy marriage.

Finally, one can receive emotional support and reassurance from the doctor in psychotherapy. At times a person needs encouragement from another human being. Pastors frequently fulfill the last three functions mentioned.

Concerning tranquilizing drugs, they are very useful at times. For instance, in cases where psychotherapy is not available a tranquilizer may give some relief from emotional suffering. When tranquilizers are used properly, they can facilitate psychotherapy by helping a patient work out a very upsetting problem. If it is used correctly there is no danger that a tranquilizer will become a crutch.

Chapter Nine

SPIRITUAL CAUSES OF NERVOUS TENSION AND PSYCHOLOGICAL DISORDERS

WE HAVE EXAMINED some physical and psychological factors involved in nervous tension. Now we come to spiritual factors that may affect a person's psychological state. Religious truths and spiritual principles are realities, and a person may react psychologically to anything that is real or that he believes to be real. Therefore the fact of God's existence may produce a psychological reaction of some type. Whereas the non-Christian has the problem of being alienated from God and thus needs to get right with God, the Christian has the need to stay on good terms with God and to have a good mental attitude toward God. He needs to have behavior patterns that do not carry him into sin and thus into conflict with God.

The following factors all have to do with mental attitudes toward spiritual matters.

Failure to Recognize God as a Person

THE PROBLEM

Many Christians know that God is the Creator and Saviour. But they fail to recognize that He is also a *person,* and therefore fail to respond to Him as a person. For instance, when a Christian realizes that everywhere he goes, the person of God goes with him and that God observes all his actions, this knowledge has a great impact on him. He realizes that he is never really alone, for God is always there with him, dwelling in him (I Cor. 6:19).

It is easy to see how our perception of God's presence will produce a great psychological effect. Not only will it make us less likely to do wrong things, but it also can make us more bold and confident to do the right things. The awareness of God's presence acts as a constant pressure on us to act in a way becoming to a Christian. The awareness of God's person (with His likes and dislikes) makes us think more about what would please or displease Him. To fail to perceive God's presence limits the spiritual benefit we can get from being a Christian. Anything that hinders our spiritual development makes us more vulnerable to upsetting stresses of ordinary life, thus more prone to nervousness.

THE REMEDY

We must accept the fact that God is a person and is always present with us. I need to point out that we cannot perceive God's presence as intensely as we can a human presence, because God does not appear to us in bodily form. We cannot see or touch God, as we can people. Yet we can understand and respond to the reality that God is with us.

Lack of Respect for the Vessel of God

THE PROBLEM

Christians are called vessels of God, in the sense of being used in service by God. (See Acts 9:15; II Cor. 4:7; II Tim. 2:21.) The body is called the temple of God the Holy Spirit (I Cor. 6:19). How then should this holy vessel be treated? Should it be abused? Should it be pressured into living in an unnatural, harmful way? Of course not. Yet many Christians fail to properly care for themselves. How can one's physical and psychological needs be ignored or refused without resulting in a weakening of the vessel?

The healthier a person is physically and psychologically, the more capable he is of understanding and applying spiritual truths to his life. We must have a reasonably clear, controlled mind to utilize spiritual principles in our life. A mind torn asunder by psychological conflict is less effective in comprehending and applying new truths.

THE REMEDY

Every Christian is obligated to keep himself in the best condition possible, both physically and psychologically. Any physical disorder should be treated and cured. Any psychological problem hindering one's effectiveness as a person should be resolved. To fail to do this shows a lack of respect for the holy vessel of God.

Paul knew of the pressures a pastor is under when he wrote Timothy to "take heed unto thyself" (literally, keep on giving attention to yourself, I Tim. 4:16). Paul's principle was that Timothy should not neglect attending to his own physical, psychological, and spiritual needs. He was not to become fatigued so that he would be unable to meet the needs of others.

To care for one's own needs requires some aggression. It means we sometimes have to assert our feelings and say no to others. This presents a problem to some people who have a mistaken idea of the meaning of the biblical recommendation to "deny self" (Matt. 16:24; Mark 8:34; Luke 9:23). To "deny self" does not mean a blanket denial of gratification of all personal needs or wishes. This would be a harsh, barren, and unnatural way of life. The proper meaning is that whenever one's personal wish conflicts with the will of God, then he is to deny himself and obey God. He denies himself in the sense that he does not put his own wishes before God's will for his life. Christians must discipline themselves to live a healthy, balanced life. At times others will demand things of us which we cannot give without bringing physical or psychological abuse upon ourselves. At these times the answer must be no. This is not selfish but wise and realistic. For example, the busy housewife must realistically limit her out-of-home activities. If she takes on too much she may become fatigued.

Another verse misinterpreted by some Christians is I Corinthians 13:5. Here Paul says that "[love] seeketh not her own [interests]. . . ." Some claim this means that it is always wrong for a Christian to insist on what he wants or needs and that he should always cater to others' needs or wishes. This is not a valid interpretation or application of this verse. Paul meant that the Christian manifesting love, in a situation where it is appropriate within God's will, will give up what he himself wants for the sake of the other person's needs. He will give up his own wish when there is a good reason for doing so, and will not insist on always having his own way. This is the balanced view. To always insist on having our own way is selfish and unloving. But to go to the other extreme and always give in to other people is foolish and unnatural and interferes with God's direction in our life. We cannot be a slave to the wishes of others and still carry out God's will for our life (Gal. 1:10).

In summary, the Christian is obligated to keep his body and mind in good condition so that he can remain useful to God.

Resisting God

THE PROBLEM

God has set up laws which regulate our lives in physical, mental and spiritual areas. When we try to live contrary to these laws we must pay the consequences.

We simply cannot get away with resisting God's laws which regulate our life. The Bible says that God "ranges into battle against" (literal translation of *antitassōmai* is "to resist") those who are proud (those who balk at obeying His laws). (See James 4:6 and I Peter 5:5).

THE REMEDY

We need to properly relate our life to God, by recognizing how He would have us live. Paul said "godliness with contentment is great gain" (I Tim. 6:6). Notice that Paul in this verse links godliness with contentment. The two are closely related. Godliness means "having the right attitude and behaving properly toward God." A godly man is one who agrees with God and tries to pattern his behavior after God. The godly man aims at living a life of obedience to God's commandments.

The author of Ecclesiastes, probably King Solomon, stated that he had tried everything that the world had to offer: wisdom, riches, pleasure, eating, labor. Yet he did not find that which satisfied his soul. In Ecclesiastes 6:7 he points out that, although man may labor, yet "the appetite (literally, soul) is not filled." His conclusion was that everything in the world not properly related to God is vanity (12:8).

Then in chapter 12:13-14 Solomon gives his conclusion as to the true way for man to find satisfaction. He says: "Let us hear the conclusion of the whole matter: Fear God, and keep his commandments: for this is the whole duty of man."

In summary, the creature cannot ignore the laws of his Creator. God has certain laws that govern the bodies, minds, and souls of men. In striving for peace of mind men must submit themselves to God, and this submission is to be manifested by obedience to His laws (James 4:7). The man who resists God will find that God resists him (James 4:6), for a refusal to submit to God's laws will result in distress of body, soul, and mind.

Failure to Yield to God

THE PROBLEM

This problem is related to the previous factor of a proper relationship to God. It has been shown that we must obey God's laws regulating our life or suffer unpleasant consequences. We are encouraged to yield ourselves to God for service (Rom. 12:1). To fail to do this may result in suffering in two ways.

First of all, if we do not yield, we are more likely to be guilty of resisting God. When self is more important than God, then we become more vulnerable to stresses and disappointments. We may become miserable, frustrated, and nervous when we cannot have our own way.

Second, if we do not yield, our relationship to God is not as close as it could be and therefore is not as rewarding and satisfying. We miss out on many benefits of Christianity when we are not yielded to God. We do not get the same power and help from Him because we are not engaged in service for Him. We do not experience all the guidance that is possible from God.

We are more likely to become involved in sin and suffer its consequences.

THE REMEDY

The concept of "yielding" is presented by Paul in Romans 12:1: "Therefore, I encourage you, brethren, by the mercies of God to present [literally, offer up for a sacrifice] your bodies a living sacrificial victim, holy, well-pleasing to God, which is your rational service" (literal, expanded translation). (See also Rom. 6:13, 19.)

The central verb in Romans 12:1 is "present" or "offer up." This word was commonly used to refer to the act where the owner of the sacrificial lamb offered up (presented) his victim to the priest for use in the Jewish worship service.

Now, in the Christian era, Paul urges every Christian, as a believer-priest (I Peter 2:9; Rev. 1:6), to offer his entire person— his body and mind—to God for the purpose of service. God wants us, as Christians, to be willing to serve Him in whatever way He asks. He has in turn promised to give us guidance and power, and to discipline us as sons, for our own good.

The book of Romans shows that the service in mind is that of living a proper Christian life, whatever this may involve. Such a life would include not only good works and adherence to a biblical moral standard, but also use of special gifts, such as preaching. The sacrifice must be "living" because only live people can be used for service. People who are dead physically have lost their usefulness in regard to earthly service. Also the person offering himself to God becomes "holy" in the sense that from then on he is "set apart" for service, much as an officer in the army is set apart for his particular duty.

This service is called rational (reasonable). The literal meaning of this word is "that which pertains to the soul or reason." This dedication to God is a conscious, rational, deliberate act. The same idea is mentioned in Ephesians 6:6 in the phrase "doing the will of God from the soul" (Grk.).

The idea of this action is illustrated today by the act of a civilian man who enlists in the army. Before one enlists he is a citizen, sympathetic to the president, the commander-in-chief of the army. But he is not carrying out orders from the chief. In fact, he is receiving few orders, if any. But after he enlists, the situation changes. At the moment of enlistment he makes a conscious, rational, deliberate decision to serve in the army of the commander-in-chief. He takes an oath in which he swears to obey the chief's orders. From then on he does not have the same freedom he had before, but is obligated to do whatever the chief commands. Similarly, once we become a soldier in God's army, we must submit to His leadership and obey His commands.

If we fail to yield to God we are more vulnerable to life's stresses and are deprived of available help from God. God gives grace to help those who are humble and yielding (James 4:6, 8a).

Sin

Without a doubt sin frequently plays a part in mental disturbances. The wicked in this world cannot expect to have true peace of mind. In Isaiah 48:22 we read: "There is no peace, saith the LORD, unto the wicked." To say that sin never has anything to do with mental disturbances is to deny God's Word.

THE PROBLEM

Sin in human experience is a fact that cannot be denied. Every human being is born into the world with a capacity and indeed a tendency to commit sin (Eph. 2:3). The Bible refers to this as the "sin nature," or the "old man," or the "flesh." Those who are not familiar with the biblical expressions explain this weakness of man as "human nature." For instance, children do not have to be taught to lie. They were born with the tendency to be deceitful. The Bible clearly indicates that the source of sin in everyone is this sin nature or capacity for sin (James 1:15).

The Bible defines sin in I John 3:4 (Williams): "Everyone who commits [keeps on practicing] sin commits lawlessness; sin is lawlessness." The translation of this verse has been expanded to bring out the meaning of the present tense. The Christian should not keep on practicing sin, but should continue to eliminate sinful habits from his life. The verse defines sin as "lawlessness," or the "breaking of God's laws." Any act of disobedience to the laws of God is sin, whether we are consciously aware of the sin or not. If the sin involves a moral law, then our inborn awareness of God's moral laws (Rom. 2:15) inevitably causes guilt.

Sin damages the soul. An exhortation to Christians is "hold yourselves back from fleshly lusts, which [lusts] are of such a nature that they carry on a continual warfare against the soul" (expanded translation of I Peter 2:11). How do lusts war against the soul? They produce sin, and sin disturbs the mind. Guilt decreases self-esteem and self-confidence and sometimes leads to undesirable behavior. It may even lead to self-punitive or self-destructive behavior. A mind damaged by sin does not function properly, and a person overburdened by sin may manifest a variety of mental symptoms such as nervousness, irritability, anxiety, depression, and poor judgment. The worse the damage, the worse the symptoms.

These three scripture verses clearly refer to the damage done to the soul by sin. The word "corrupt" is used (a translation of the Greek word *phtheirō*) to mean "to ruin something by a process of corruption."

(1) Ephesians 4:22: "Put off . . . the old man which is being progressively corrupted by the action of the lusts of deceit."

(2) II Peter 1:4: "Having escaped the moral degeneration [corruption] which [is] in the world because of lusts."

(3) Galatians 6:8 warns: "He who sows to the flesh [the sin nature] shall reap corruption from the flesh."

In Revelation 19:2 God uses this same word for "corrupt" when He executes judgment upon the great harlot who "ruined by a process of corruption the earth" with her fornication. (This refers to the corruption of the earth by idolatrous religion.)

This same word is also used twice in I Corinthians 3:17, referring to a Christian who misbehaves and thus corrupts the Christian assembly. The Christian, because he has God's Holy Spirit within him and should be holy, is called the "temple of the Holy Spirit" (I Cor. 6:19). In I Corinthians 3:16 the Christian assembly is also referred to as God's temple. In I Corinthians

3:17 it says, "If someone defiles [ruins by corrupting] the temple of God, this one God shall defile [ruin by corrupting]." In other words, God will see to it that the one who corrupts the temple of God, whether his own person or the assembly, will also suffer the judgment of corruption. This corruption may result in nervous symptoms when the mind is affected. God promises to the Christian, as well as to the non-Christian, that sin pays a salary—the process of moral degeneration of the soul (Prov. 6:32; 8:36).

We can clearly see the effects of this damage upon the mind in the life of one who has knowingly practiced sin for a long time. A prostitute who has practiced her trade for many years often looks corrupt. Something has eaten out her soul.

The Bible indicates some of the specific damaging effects that sin will produce upon the mind. I Timothy 4:2 speaks of a person's conscience being seared (literally, branded), referring to the weakening effect of sin upon the conscience. When a person sins once, his conscience usually bothers him. But after the second time, and the third, and so on, he becomes hardened, and eventually feels no apparent twinge of conscience at all. His conscience has been damaged to the point that it no longer functions as it should. That is why Peter exhorts Christians to maintain "a good conscience" (I Peter 3:16).

In I John 2:11 it says that sin (here called walking in darkness instead of in the light), when practiced long enough, results in spiritual blindness, which lowers or eliminates the Christian's ability to perceive new truth and to see his own faults. This is a dangerous condition for one who desires to maintain good mental health. We have to be able to see the sin in our lives in order to handle it properly. We have to be aware of our faults before we can improve ourselves. Otherwise we will continue making the same mistakes, committing the same sins, which will cause damage to the soul.

In addition the Bible mentions slavery as a third result of the practice of sin. In II Peter 2:19 it says that when we give ourselves up to and are overcome by a particular lust (or bad habit), we become enslaved by it. We see about us today the chronic alcoholic who longs to give up his drinking but cannot; the smoker who longs to give up his cigarettes but cannot; the glutton who longs to be able to eat less and lose his excess weight but cannot. The alcoholic is a slave to his liquor, the smoker to his cigarettes, and the glutton to his appetite. Although each may feel that what he is doing is wrong, because he is enslaved to his habit, he cannot quit.

It is easy to see how a soul damaged by sin can be subject to mental breakdown and disease. However, we should not conclude that the factor of sin is involved in every case of mental illness in a Christian. We must not make the mistake of Job's friends who "found no answer, and yet . . . condemned Job" (Job 32:3). The Bible clearly states that it was the Lord who brought the evil upon Job (Job 42:11) and not Job who brought it upon himself.

In some cases sin is a major cause of mental illness. A mental breakdown may be the result of living in known sin over an extended period of time. The Christian's conscience may have informed him of his sin, and yet he continued in it anyway, experiencing guilt and anxiety.

Sin is deceiving, and the painful results of the sin may not be evident at first. But suffering is inevitable, even though it may take a while for the effect of the damage to show up. A Christian may not realize just how weakened he has become from the practice of sin until some test or trial, some storm of life, comes along. Then he may crumble and break down.

A ship which is badly damaged and in need of repairs can sail on the open sea and get along well until a storm blows up. Then what happens? The ship cannot take it and ends up a wreck. (The very term "shipwreck" is used by Paul in I Tim. 1:19.) It takes a test to expose the weakness of the ship. Likewise a person weakened by sin may seem to do pretty well, until a storm comes along and he breaks down.

THE REMEDY

Since none of us will ever be without some sin in this life, we must learn the remedy for it. Christ has provided a remedy to protect the Christian from the damaging effects of sin. A basic truth to realize is that, on the basis of Christ's death for sinners, the Christian has been freed from the dominion of the sin nature (see Romans 6). This means that we can will to obey God instead of the sin nature. Now we can determine in our hearts to be a bondslave of God, instead of a slave to the sin nature.

However, as we struggle (with the help of God's power, of course) to throw off our old habits of sin, we find that frequently, before we have completely conquered a particular sinful habit, we fail many times. We do not want to fail, but the flesh is weak and we find ourselves falling into sin. Christians are not perfect, and must still strive to overcome sin and its damaging effects on the soul.

The remedy which God has provided to protect us from this damage is cleansing. God promises cleansing from the corrupting effects of sin, *if we walk in the light* (I John 1:7).

What does it mean to walk in the light? "Light" is God's truth which shows us the right way to live as a Christian. To be "in the light" means to have knowledge of the right way to live as a Christian. It is the opposite of being in the dark. To "walk in the light" means to live a life of obedience to the truth of God's Word. In order to do this we must: (1) know the truth, and (2) obey the truth.

Does "walking in the light" mean sinless perfection, a life without sin? No. God recognizes that Christians will fail. He knows that even the best Christian, one who is trying hard to obey God's Word, will sometimes fail and sin (I John 1:8, 10). Can we commit sin and still walk in the light? Yes, if we do what the light tells us to do about our sin.

What does the light tell us to do about our sin? It tells us to "confess" (I John 1:9). So walking in the light means: (1) obeying all God's commandments, and (2) confessing our failures to obey.

What is confession? It does not mean simply telling God about your sin. He already knows all about it. To confess means to "agree with God" about your sin. The Greek word translated "confess" means to "agree with." Confession means "taking God's attitude toward sin." What is God's attitude toward sin? He hates sin, and you will hate it too, if you agree with Him about it. God wants you to have the victory over that sinful habit so that you can stop committing that sin. You also should have this goal. God also wants you to ask Him for the power to overcome that sin and wants you to keep on trying, with His help, to overcome it. If you agree with Him about it, then you will also want to keep struggling against sin and you will keep on praying to Him for help. All this is part of confession.

Overcoming a sinful habit may involve the resolution of a psychological problem underlying the habit. A sin may be the symptom of a psychological problem. The problem causes the sinful tendency to repeatedly return.

"Walking in the light" involves our heart attitude toward the whole law of God, not just toward our sin. It is walking in obedience to God's laws that guarantees cleansing from sin. The Christian who fails to make "walking in the light" the practice of his life will undoubtedly be damaged by sin, and may develop mental illness. In this case what remedy will relieve the damage produced by sin? There is no remedy other than to go ahead and reap the consequences. When the full crop has been reaped (and this may take months or years), then improvement will occur. It is imperative that the Christian stop sowing sin, or he will never stop reaping until he dies. And there may be little improvement in his mental condition until he has finished the reaping time.

When he stops sowing the sin, confesses it, and begins walking in the light, then after a time, perhaps months later when the full crop has been reaped, improvement will occur. During the time of reaping there is little or nothing that can remove the effects of sin. The damage has been done and must run its course. The counseling pastor must encourage the Christian patient to wait patiently until the reaping has ended. He can assure the patient that he will enjoy better mental health after this process is completed.

I feel that sometimes such a huge crop of sins has been sown that the reaping cannot be completed within the lifetime of the patient. If he has damaged his soul too greatly, he may never in this life regain good mental health. This is a most solemn thought. Be careful what you sow and cultivate in the garden of your life. That which you sow and cultivate is exactly what you will reap later on.

Failure to Obey the Conscience

THE PROBLEM

Acting contrary to the convictions of the conscience can be sin. It defiles the person and is mentally disturbing because of the guilt it creates (Rom. 14:23; I Cor. 8:7, 12). A person can be tortured by the pangs of a guilty conscience, and this may damage the mind. It is quite important to have a healthy conscience and to obey it.

Paul, in I Timothy 1:19, shows that the failure to maintain a good conscience is a causative factor in a Christian's becoming shipwrecked. We must determine from a study of this passage what Paul meant by the term "shipwreck."

First, in verse 18, Timothy is told to wage a good warfare. Timothy's warfare was being an obedient Christian and carrying on his ministry, which in his case was being the pastor of a church. In verse 19 Paul gives the manner or method by which he is to wage this warfare. Assuming that the present participle *holding* is a modal participle, it is better translated "maintaining." Timothy is told to wage a good warfare by maintaining two things: (1) *faith*, that is, living by faith, and (2) a *good conscience*. It is not "the faith," that is, the body of Christian truth, which is in view. The word "faith" does not have the article *the* before it, indicating that it is the principle of faith, or "living by faith."

Then Paul points out that "some, as a result of having put away faith and a good conscience, have suffered shipwreck in regard to their faith." Here the word "faith" means their Christian career. These men put away (literally, thrust away from themselves) the principles of living by faith and of maintaining a good conscience. As a result, they may have developed some sort of breakdown, some deterioration in their character; a weakening of their psychological and spiritual condition. The case of a ship undergoing shipwreck perfectly illustrates what happened to them as Christians. This same word is used in II Corinthians 11:25 where it refers to an actual shipwreck. Two things happen in a Christian's shipwreck: (1) The course that was plotted or intended is interrupted, and (2) he is in no condition to function properly as a Christian while he is in such a condition. He must be repaired (as a ship is repaired in dry dock) before he can again act as a Christian should.

Notice also in I Timothy 1:20 that Paul mentions that these two men were delivered up to Satan so that they might be taught to stop blaspheming. Blasphemy means to "regard lightly" or "speak lightly of" or "despise" that which is holy. A Christian who refuses to live by faith and maintain a good conscience is a "blasphemer" in that he has regarded lightly and despised the commandments of God.

In this case the two blasphemers suffered from Satan, who attacked them, acting as God's agent of chastening. An attack by Satan can be a factor in some cases of mental disorders in Christians. These verses demonstrate how several factors may operate in unison to result in a breakdown.

The conscience itself deserves special discussion. The conscience can be (1) ignorant (thus failing to inform us before we sin) or (2) underdeveloped (thus failing to hold us back from sin), or (3) seared (thus failing to function consciously in certain areas), or (4) overly strict (thus making us feel guilty when we have not sinned or feel excessive guilt when we do sin).

Let us consider the problem of an ignorant conscience. The conscience will register a protest whenever the Christian considers doing or does something which violates a basic moral law or a known scriptural principle. I use the term "known" scriptural principle because to a certain extent the conscience is limited to one's knowledge of the truth. There are certain acts which seem to be intuitively recognized as morally wrong. These sins involve a violation of one of God's eternal moral laws. Such sins as: incest, murder, lying, adultery, and stealing would be in this category. But many other wrongs must be learned. The con-

science, as a function of the mind, is not always right, and is sometimes weak (I Cor. 8:7). This means that it does not always have
the correct information and needs to be reeducated. This reeducation of the conscience is important. It is accomplished by
acquiring a knowledge of the Bible.

Also the conscience should be oriented primarily toward God
(Acts 24:16), and not merely toward men. Men do not always
see what we do, but God does. We need to remind ourselves
that God (Prov. 15:3; Heb. 4:13) and the angels (I Cor. 4:9) are
our spectators.

Furthermore, there is a danger in trying too hard to please
men so as not to offend them. The danger is that we may become
prisoners to the illogical and irrational prejudices of other people.
To become enslaved to the opinions of others in this way makes
it difficult for our minds to be free to function in a rational and
logical way. A Christian trying to make a decision about God's
will for his life must reason logically about it, using all the facts
he has. He must be able to think intelligently for himself. To be
bound to what others think makes him a slave to others. Such a
person cannot be a servant (literally, bondslave) of Christ (Gal.
1:10). Our first responsibility is to God, even though men may
be offended by an act of obedience to God. Paul warns us against
being misled by the judgments of other men (Col. 2:16-18).

Paul mentions the seared conscience in I Timothy 4:2. The
word "seared" literally means "branded." This term suggests that
the conscience, while not being totally destroyed, has been damaged so that it will not function in regard to conviction about certain sins. Although at first the conscience will convict about that
sin, when the sin is repeated over and over without being confessed then the voice of the conscience becomes weaker and
weaker until finally it is not heard at all. The conscience is damaged (seared) so that it cannot make itself heard whenever that
particular sin is committed. The verb *branded* is in the Greek
perfect tense, which suggests "a permanent injury which produces
lasting results."

As to the underdeveloped conscience, this is often a psychological problem. It may stem from childhood problems, especially from an environment where the child never had a close love relationship with anyone who really accepted him as a person. The fear of displeasing a loved one is a normal and important factor in developing a good healthy conscience. If the child has no one who really loves him then he feels he will lose nothing by his misbehavior. Therefore he fails to develop sufficient self-control to avoid doing wrong. Discipline is necessary for a child, but it must be preceded by and combined with love.

An underdeveloped conscience may also result from loose parental discipline. A parent who is too easy on his child and lets him have his way too often is really not helping him. It is necessary to set reasonable limits upon a child's behavior. A child who has seldom been disciplined may grow into an adult who has trouble controlling himself. His conscience may tell him he should not do something, but this is not sufficient to keep him from doing it. He lacks self-control.

In regard to the overly strict conscience, Paul describes this as a "weak" conscience (I Cor. 8:7). It is weak in that it convicts the person of sin when he really has not sinned, thus producing an unnecessarily restricted life. This is also a common psychological problem. This type of conscience may result from too much environmental criticism during childhood. Perhaps as a child he was unable to please his parents, as they gave him too much criticism and not enough praise. Later, as an adult, he may find himself doubting that he can do anything right. He may still fear that he will be criticized for what he does, so he is afraid to do anything. Every decision he makes is followed by doubts as to whether it is right. As a Christian, such a person doubts many of the decisions he makes about the Lord's will, even though he may have made the right decision. So we must consider what our conscience says, but it should not have life or death veto power over our decisions.

The Christian with an overly strict conscience holds back, unsure of himself. He is doubtful and is reluctant to go ahead with a decision about the Lord's will. The Christian with an underdeveloped conscience rushes ahead too quickly, often rashly and incorrectly. The desirable balance must be found between these two extremes.

THE REMEDY

The obvious way to avoid trouble is to maintain a good conscience and obey it (Rom. 14:5, 23; I Peter 3:16). When a sin is committed it should be confessed (I John 1:9). But when the conscience is damaged, it is too late for preventative measures. Each problem mentioned has a specific remedy. For example, the ignorant conscience needs to be reeducated in the knowledge of the Word of God. The seared conscience is a difficult problem. I know of no promise in the Bible in which God says He will undo this. Intensive psychiatric treatment might help some by uncovering some subconscious guilt feelings which could be mobilized to influence the person to stop his misbehavior.

The underdeveloped conscience can be treated psychiatrically. This is often the problem—in extreme form—of the so-called psychopath. Successful treatment must be intense and in a controlled atmosphere (such as an institution) where the psychopath and his environment can be controlled.

The overly strict conscience can be helped more easily. Psychiatric therapy may help make a conscience less strict. The person needs to learn to pay less attention to the overly strict, illogical side of his conscience. A true warning from God through the conscience is neither illogical nor irrational. If he is trusting in God to energize him to want the Lord's will, he can train himself to ignore the irrational doubts that stem from his abnormal conscience.

One rule that should be noted in evaluating what the conscience says is: When the action advised by the conscience is correct, it will always be based clearly upon some moral or scriptural principle. We should always be able to point to some verse in the Bible which legitimately supports the claim of the conscience. However, if the conscience says: "It's wrong but I can't tell you why," and there never does emerge any legitimate reason why it would be wrong, the conscience may be overly strict, or the conclusion of the conscience may be based on a prejudice. If it is God warning us against a decision, He usually uses the truth of the Word of God. A vague, inappropriate, irrational doubt is not from God but from an overly strict or misinformed conscience.

It is true that "whatsoever is not of faith is sin" (Rom. 14:23). But an irrational doubt does not prove that an act is not of faith. The irrational doubt must be recognized for what it is—a symptom of a psychological problem—that of an overly strict conscience. Actions which we regard as "of faith" should be based on our knowledge of the truth, because our feelings can often fool us.

Thus we need to educate and obey our conscience. If we do not obey it, it will make us miserable. If we persist in disobeying it, then our conscience will become weakened to the point of not functioning properly. It will fail to warn us when we are doing something wrong. This results in even more sin and trouble.

Weakness of Man

THE PROBLEM

The weakness of man makes him susceptible to breakdown whenever a sufficiently heavy strain is put upon him. He tends to tire and become exhausted if he tries to do too much work in one day. Sometimes a Christian tries to perform some ministry or service for the Lord and finds that his work is hindered by his own weakness and limitations.

Why has God made us weak? The answer is II Corinthians 4:7. Even though we are Christians we are still "vessels of clay," in order that the "preeminence of the power [literally, ability] may be from God, and not from us." If we could go through life without getting tired and fatigued, without ever failing; if we could perform our ministry without any problems; if we could serve without conscious awareness of our need of help from God; then we could also take the glory. But God deserves the glory, and He has deliberately chosen to work through weak vessels. God enables us to do what He commands and furnishes what is needed for the performance of the service.

How weak are we? Unless we engage in a certain amount of

work, sleep, relaxation, and wholesome activity, we tend to become unbalanced, sick, fatigued, and may eventually break down. Furthermore, the Christian has an extremely high standard of behavior toward which he aims. Although he cannot achieve perfect adherence to this standard in this life, yet he strives toward this goal. What happens when the Christian tries to live up to this high standard while depending upon and using only his own natural ability—the "energy of the flesh"? He finds that the flesh is weak and fails. "The spirit indeed is willing, but the flesh is weak" (Matt. 26:41).

When a Christian keeps on striving and straining with his own energy to live up to this high standard, yet constantly fails, this results in fatigue and frustration, two things that are damaging to the mind. God sometimes allows the Christian to experience failure so that he may learn the lesson that he must depend upon God for the power to live the Christian life, and not merely rely upon his own energy and ability (II Cor. 1:8-9).

When a Christian refuses to admit his weakness and does not recognize his need for God's power, then he may keep on trying harder and harder and straining more and more, until finally he has a breakdown. To such a person a nervous breakdown can be a blessing, if through it he is convinced that he must not depend solely upon his own energy to live the Christian life. Only when he comes to the point where he realizes his need of God's enabling power will he be willing and able to receive God's provision for his weakness. Paul learned this lesson. Writing to the Corinthians he said, "We were pressed . . . even to the point of despair . . ." (II Cor. 1:8-9). Why? In order that "we should not trust in ourselves, but in God." In Philippians 3:3 Paul said, "We are . . . they who . . . are not trusting in [the] flesh." In Romans 7:18 Paul said that "In me [that is, in my flesh], good does not dwell." In verse 21 Paul admitted that there is a law, the law of the indwelling sin nature (that human tendency to do the wrong thing), which exerts a constant pressure upon the Christian in such a way that he tends to sin, doing that which he does not want to do.

Those who strive to live up to the Christian standard using

their own natural ability carry a heavy load, a great burden, a yoke which they are not able to bear (Acts 15:10; Gal. 3:3). They feel the strain upon themselves acutely, and frequently complain that it is hard to live the Christian life and that the commandments of God are "grievous" (hard to obey), even though the Bible says that they are not (I John 5:3). To rely solely upon one's own natural energy, without depending upon God's help, will result in frequent spiritual failures. These failures bring a sense of frustration and guilt. At times there is an up-and-down struggle over a particular sin. Paul gives evidence of such a struggle in Romans 7.

THE REMEDY

Paul gives the remedy in Romans 8:4. He refers to victorious Christians as those "who do not walk according to the flesh but according to the Spirit." The answer is to live in conscious dependence upon the power available from God the Holy Spirit. The Spirit will supply us with power to live the Christian life as we depend upon Him.

When we rely on the Spirit, in a sense we enter into *rest*. We rest from our own works, that is, doing works in our own energy. Hebrews 4:10 points out that the one who enters into rest "hath ceased from his own works." He has stopped striving and straining to perform good works in the energy of the flesh. Instead he has started trusting God to supply him with the energy and ability to live up to the Christian standard.

To enter into rest does not mean that we sit down and do nothing. What we do now is to consciously try to do the right thing, relying on God to supply the power. He may not do this immediately. There may be a temporary struggle involved while we strive to master the problem. But He will help us gain victory over our problem if we wait for His help. (See Phil. 2:13 and Col. 1:29; also Ps. 37:3-7, 17, 23-24, 34, 39; 145:18-20; Prov. 3:5.)

We must also make use of the remedies which He provides. For the mind which needs to be refreshed, this empowering ministry of God the Holy Spirit supplies refreshment. We are promised such a ministry by God in Ephesians 4:23, "constantly being renewed in regard to the spirit of your mind," and Colossians 3:10 "the new man, which is constantly being renewed." (See also Ps. 23:3; 34:22.)

But this renewing of the Christian's mind comes to pass only as he comes to God and admits his need to being refreshed and asks God for help. (See Ps. 2:12; 62:2, 8; 107:9; 138:3.) In Matthew 11:28 Christ said, "Come to me, all ye who labor and are weary with burdens [those who feel burdened with sin and desire salvation], and I myself will rejuvenate you." Here the phrase "give you rest" means "cause someone to become refreshed by stopping his labor." In verse 29 Christ says, "Take my yoke upon you . . . and you will find rejuvenation for your souls." Christ was here issuing an invitation to those who were weary of their burden of guilt over sin to trust in Him for their salvation. He continued to point out that the Christian life after salvation is not a hard, burdensome thing. He said "my yoke is mild and my burden is light [literally, easy to bear]" (Matt. 11:30). The "yoke" here is the body of God's commandments, the high Christian standard. It can be easy to bear because God helps a Christian live up to this standard when he habitually trusts in Him to supply the power.

Paul in Colossians 1:29 stated that in his ministry he was consciously laboring and constantly combating. But it was according to God's power "which was constantly energizing him mightily" (literally, with ability). The word for *power* in this verse is the word for operative power. From it we get our word *energy*. Notice we are to consciously use all the energy we have, but we are also to be consciously trusting that God's power will supply that energy. In Colossians 1:11 Paul points out that the Christian who is trying to live a godly life and is trusting God for the power to do so is "constantly being empowered with every ability . . . unto patient endurance and longsuffering with joy."

Thus the Christian who labors in his Christian life by the energy of the Holy Spirit will not run out of energy for the performance of that which is God's will. When the energy runs out, that is an indication that God's enabling power has been turned off; it is time to rest until the next day when God will supply more power for the new day's work.

When the Christian continually tries to serve God in the energy of the flesh, he will become tired and fatigued, and the pressure can contribute to the development of a breakdown. I can illustrate this by citing a frequent occurrence in the life of a Christian student. I had several years of study at seminary, and I know what it is like to attend school, work after school, and then try to study at night, still finding time for sleep, rest, and relaxation. If a student is yielded to the Spirit, his whole life, including his study life, his work life, and his sleep life, is being directed by the Spirit. So the student tackles the night's homework, perhaps working until ten or eleven at night, when his body and mind are tired. To continue to study after the mind is exhausted is to abuse it. The Holy Spirit usually does not lead a Christian to do that which is abusive to his mind or body. The Christian student should stop and go to bed, so that the next day his mind will be rested and will be responsive to God's directions.

But the student immediately objects and says, "Oh, but I can't stop now; I have a test tomorrow." Or if not a test, it is a paper that is due, or something else that just has to be done. If the student goes on working and studying after God the Holy Spirit, through the student's fatigue, has told him to go to bed, then he is working and studying in the energy of the flesh, rather than the Spirit. God the Holy Spirit energizes the Christian to do only that which is His will, not that which is contrary to His will.

If the student stays up, out of the will of God, and labors in his own energy, he may get through his test with a passing grade, or maybe even an A. It may seem at first that studying in the energy of the flesh works well. This is deceiving. After a while he may find himself having to push himself each night in order to do the required studying. He may discover that he has lost the drive and energy that the Holy Spirit had been giving him. Now he has to study all the time in the energy of the flesh, and it becomes increasingly difficult.

What has happened? Well, for one thing he has sinned against the Holy Spirit by refusing to go to bed when God told him to. This has probably not been confessed and cleared up. Also he is developing fatigue, that dangerous enemy of the mind. Finally, he has begun cultivating a new habit—the habit of studying in the energy of the flesh. After having practiced this for some time, sooner or later he will begin to reap the consequences. What are the consequences? Fatigue, tiredness, a spiritual dullness and coldness, a slowing of spiritual interest. And if he drives himself too hard and too long, there is danger of a breakdown.

The Christian student should study as hard as possible for as long as God enables him. But when he realizes that God has withdrawn His enabling power for the evening and he becomes tired and fatigued, then it is time to quit and get some rest. Let God handle the problem of the test the next day. The Christian must not abuse the vessel through which the Lord is working. Every Christian, whether a student, housewife, or businessman, should let the Holy Spirit plan his day. He will enable you to do what is God's will for the day.

The Effect of the World upon the Christian

The Problem

By "the world" I refer to that system of life which includes people, things, moral values, ideals, goals, and practices that are contrary to God, or ungodly. This world system is an ever-present enemy of the Christian. Christ in John 15:18-20 makes it clear that this world system is opposed to the Christian. The Apostle John, in I John 2:15-17, points out that this world system is not "of the Father" and is therefore different from and contrary to God. This world system concerns itself with those things that will satisfy the "lust of the flesh, and the lust of the eyes, and the pride of life" (I John 2:16).

Furthermore, the world today is the same one which hated and murdered our Lord Jesus Christ. Today it looks at the fervent Christian with hostility and resentment. Therefore, if the Christian tries to live as he should in this ungodly world, he can expect the world to treat him just as it treated Christ, with hatred and persecution (Gal. 4:29; I John 3:1, 13). James makes it clear that the friendship with the world is enmity with God and that anyone who makes up his mind to be a friend of the world is rendered an "enemy of God" (James 4:4).

Now the Christian must be victorious over the world, or the world will overpower him in such a way as to nullify his Christian testimony. In I John 5:4-5, John points out that there is a close relationship between the principle of walking by faith and a Christian's victory over the world. The world exerts tremendous pressure upon the Christian to make him conform to its standard. The Christian businessman, for instance, feels the pressure of the world's lack of honesty and integrity when he has to compete against other businessmen who are dishonest and unscrupulous. If he is honest he may have to resign himself to losing a certain amount of business. The Christian salesman who will not drink, curse, carouse and be "one of the boys" can expect to lose some sales, and sometimes lose his job.

Socially, the world has no interest in what appears to be a straight-laced, puritanical, killjoy who will not go along with the crowd. And the Christian cannot follow the crowd, or he will fall into sin. Religiously, the world wants no part of the Christian who preaches a gospel of salvation by grace and who adds that true conversion to Christ will usually result in a change of life—away from the wicked ways of sin toward the obedience of the way of righteousness.

Christ Himself said in Matthew 7:14 that the gate that leads into eternal life is narrow; and that the way of righteousness, after one has entered through the gate and is on his way to heaven, is a narrow (literally, compressed) way. This way (road) is hedged in by many fences and walls which direct the Christian. When a person by faith becomes a child of God and enters God's family he is restricted by many commandments, both dos and don'ts, which do not permit him to continue in his life of unrestricted sin. If he does persist in this kind of life, he may receive chastening from God.

The world does not like this narrow way of living. It chooses the broad way which leads to destruction (Matt. 7:13). It also ridicules and persecutes the Christian who no longer goes along with it in its sin (I Peter 4:3-4). Today the world considers it a virtue to be "broad-minded" about everything, including sin. But God does not consider this attitude a virtue. The Christian will frequently find that, if he is obedient in his life and ministry for the Lord, he may not be able to enjoy many of the luxuries of this world, and he may experience hardships (II Tim. 2:3). A Christian who desires to be effective for the Lord cannot allow himself to become too involved or entangled in the affairs of this world or he will be hindered in his service to God (v. 4). It is a spiritual tragedy today that the Christian businessman who works hard to earn his money often seems to lack the time and energy to engage in serious Bible study, regular meditation and prayer with God. Perhaps it would be better for such a Christian to be satisfied with a little less money and a lower living standard if this would permit him more time for God and His Word. For him to lower his standard of living for God, however, would be utter foolishness from the world's viewpoint.

Many things about this world system put pressure upon the Christian to live opposite to the teaching of God's laws. Yet the Christian cannot expect God's blessing upon his life unless he lives a life of obedience. Neither will there be as many rewards in heaven unless there has been obedience during the life on earth (II Tim. 2:5).

Today the pace of the world is faster than ever. Big business is bigger. It is the accepted custom for a man today to buy a house on the basis of his earning capacity for the next twenty years. This means that his paycheck for the next twenty years is already appointed for spending. Of course, along with the house comes the accompanying worry and anxiety about what would happen if he should lose his earning capacity. Even with insurance, the thought of all these threatening possibilities can produce great tension and increased pressure.

Paul in Romans 12:2 says to Christians, "Stop being conformed to this world." This means not to be conformed to the world's pattern or mold. Peter used the same word in I Peter 1:14: "not fashioning yourselves." Instead of conforming to the world's pattern, Paul tells us to "keep on becoming transformed by the renewing of your mind" (Rom. 12:2). In I Peter 1:15-16 it says,

"Be ye holy." How can the Christian do this in the face of the pressure of the world? How can he be victorious over the world system which may persecute him for refusing to conform?

Now the world is not irreligious. In fact it has many gods, but it does not know the true God (Eph. 2:12). It worships such gods as money, power, and beauty. And the pressure of today's living is definitely a factor in the development of tension and nervousness. Christians often find the pressure crushing, for the world is hard on the Christian or anyone who refuses to conform and go along with the crowd. How can he be victorious over this pressure?

THE REMEDY

The only way that the Christian can be victorious is to "walk by faith" (I John 5:4-5). What does it mean to walk by faith? It means to let that which God has said in His Word (not what the world says) become the ruling and guiding standard in his life. The Word of God should govern our final decisions in life. If God's Word clearly says to do something, then we should do it in spite of the consequences, trusting that God will honor obedience to His Word.

Sometimes God may lead the Christian to do something that the world would consider utterly foolish, perhaps poor business. If we do what God wants us to in face of the world's warnings about the dire consequences, then we have to do it by faith. The Christian who feels led by God to give his last dollar to a missionary, not knowing where he will get money for food the next day, can do this only by faith. The world would judge it ridiculous for him to give away his last dollar, leaving no reserve in case of emergency. But the Christian walks by faith. If he were walking by sight he could not release his last dollar without great fear, because his lack of money would cause great distress. He would be especially anxious if he were without a source of security, such as a bank account. Of course it is not wrong to have a reserve of money, but this reserve should not be given life or death importance.

The Christian who is told by God to give his last dollar to the

Lord's work should give it and trust that God will enable him to obtain food for the next day. He must ignore what the world warns about the dangers of such a move and give by faith. Faith assures that God will solve all the problems that develop as a result of the Christian's obedience to the will of God.

If the Christian does not want to be plagued by worry and anxiety, he must "walk by faith," not by sight. If he insists on "walking by sight," then sooner or later what he sees and trusts in will fail, and so will he. If he is trusting in his bank account, he begins to worry about inflation. Or if he owns property, he worries about an approaching depression. If he is trusting in his job, then he fears he may lose it. There are many unpleasant experiences in life, but the Christian should not become overly anxious and worried. This is an act of disobedience and sin and results in unrest of mind (see Matt. 6:25-34; Phil. 4:6-7).

Paul warns the rich not to "trust in uncertain riches, but the living God . . ." (I Tim. 6:17). Why not trust in riches? Because they are uncertain and will fail. I Timothy 6:10 points out that the love of money is a root of all kinds of evil, and that the Christian who covets money errs from the faith and pierces himself through with many sorrows.

Paul has also warned in I Timothy 1:19 that a shipwreck can occur in the life of any Christian who does not live by faith. If you, as a Christian, persist in living by sight and trust too heavily in the material things of this world, then when these fail and some storm of life comes along, you will be unprepared to weather it. You may have a shipwreck, or a nervous breakdown.

What should a Christian specifically set his hope upon and his trust in? Both I Peter 1:13 and II Timothy 2:1 emphasize that we should have our hope fixed upon the *grace of God*. II Peter 1:4 points out that it is through the agency of the promises of God that we become "sharers in the divine nature and escape the moral degeneration which is in the world." God in grace has given us many promises of providing for the needs in this life (e.g., Phil. 4:19). In I Peter 2:6 is the astounding statement that "he who is resting his faith upon Him shall positively never be disappointed." This verse compares our trust in Him with a building that rests upon a solid foundation. If the foundation is good, then the building is solid and secure and can weather any storm.

Many Christians today have all their investments in earthly things. They spend too much of their time figuring out how to make more money and how to spend the money they have. They become worried and sick because of financial loss. The stock market goes up, and then down; previously valuable real estate becomes worthless when a highway is rerouted; or what seemed to be a good business deal does not work out. When these things happen, the Christian whose attention and affection is centered upon financial gain develops undue anxiety. What should he expect from this untrustworthy world? (See I Tim. 6:17.)

The things of this world are corruptible (I Peter 1:18), and as they degenerate and become worthless, the Christian who has cherished them will undergo mental suffering. Some thoughtful planning for material needs is necessary, but overemphasis on material possessions is a form of greed.

The remedy is to walk by faith and not by sight. Faith tells us to have our attention fastened upon things that are unseen rather than seen (II Cor. 4:18). We are to keep our affection fastened upon the things of Christ and heaven (Heb. 12:2; Col. 3:1-2), and to keep on fighting the good fight of faith (I Tim. 6:12). To do all this we must walk by faith instead of by sight (II Cor. 5:7).

The Word of God will never fail us, and that is why the author of Hebrews (6:19) tells us that in Christ we have an *anchor* for the soul that is *sure* (literally, will not slip) and *steadfast* (literally, firm, "will not lose its grip"). A boat with an anchor will not be driven onto the rocks by the storms and end up shipwrecked.

The Christian should have his trust firmly fixed upon Christ, who will serve as an Anchor for his soul; then the storms and uncertainties of life will not shipwreck him.

Failure to Put First Things First

THE PROBLEM

Whenever a man allows something to become important to him he is vulnerable to disappointment and depression. For example, if he lets himself fall in love with a woman, then she becomes important and he will be unhappy unless he can have her with him. Or if he lets money become very important to him he will be unhappy unless he has plenty of it. We need to give careful thought to that which we set our heart on. Christ said that a person's heart is where his treasure is (Matt. 6:21). This is another way of saying that a person tends to seek after and accumulate that which is most important to him.

If we put as first in importance the material things of this life (such as money, clothes, food, luxuries, etc.) then we have made a mistake for several reasons. Notice I am not saying such things are unimportant. I am speaking of the error of making them too important. What are the reasons?

First, material things are uncertain and perishable (Matt. 6:19; I Tim. 6:17; I Peter 1:18). They can easily be lost, thus plunging the owner into a state of disappointment and depression over his loss (Prov. 11:28).

Second, to put such things first in importance is to invest more mental energy in them than they deserve. It represents a waste of valuable energy (Matt. 6:27). It is unnecessary to spend much valuable time and thought worrying over material things. Why? Because God habitually clothes and feeds the animal and plant kingdoms and logically would do the same thing for the human race (vv. 26, 28, 30). God knows we need these things (v. 32), therefore we should not become overly anxious about them (Phil. 4:6). (The normal amount of concern that motivates a person to perform constructive and worthwhile labor to earn his living is not in view here).

Third, if we place material things first in importance we become enslaved to them—they become our master (Matt. 6:24). When one is addicted to something, it makes him vulnerable to the emotional suffering that is bound to come when the desired object is lost. We are not to be slaves to money, for example. Money should be only a means to an end, not an end in itself. We should be masters of our money, using it for worthwhile goals, not letting it master us.

Paul mentioned the emotional conflict that develops when our human nature seeks to put material things first while the Holy Spirit is working to elevate spiritual things to first place (Gal. 5:17). There is a competition between our human nature and the Holy Spirit at these times.

The Remedy

The obvious remedy is to put the most important things first. Christ said we should become concerned about the earning of rewards (treasures) in heaven, since we cannot lose those rewards (Matt. 6:20). Christ recommended putting God's program and God's righteousness first since God would provide for our material needs (Matt. 6:33). In other words we should rank spiritual things first in importance and material things should be of secondary concern (Col. 3:1-2). We should not be as those whom Paul criticized because their primary interest was in earthly things (Phil. 3:18-19).

If we give top priority to spiritual things then we do not experience such intense depression over losing material possessions. And our heavenly treasures are safe and secure since the power of God safeguards them.

Failure to Eliminate Thorns

The Problem

This has been discussed as a factor which hinders spiritual maturity. It is mentioned again because it is such a serious factor in developing mental illness. If we allow material things or earthly matters to become too important to us, we will experience continued pressure which can produce dissatisfaction, unhappiness and depression.

The Remedy

An increased effort at making money is a cure only when one's present standard of living is abnormally low. Otherwise the Christian should learn to live within his own means. To be able to adjust one's expectations and wishes to a realistic level is a sign of both psychological and spiritual maturity.

Failure to Eliminate Weights

THE PROBLEM

Weights have also been mentioned before under spiritual maturity. I refer to them again to make clear the psychological principle involved. Weights become injurious when they drain off energy and time, preventing full effectiveness. For example, a mother who needs and wants to spend time with her own children should not permit her time to be monopolized by overtalkative neighbors who visit too much. The visiting may be fun, but is unnecessary. And it puts pressure on the mother who feels she is neglecting her children and experiences frustration.

THE REMEDY

The expenditures of our time and energy should be goal-directed. The goals should be our goals and not those of others. We should drive toward the goals to which God has directed us and not to those which our neighbors and friends think we ought to have. If God wants you to visit your own child and a friend requests you to visit with her instead, you should say no to the friend and explain why. If your friend gets angry because you will not cater to her wants, then she is wrong. Perhaps you are better off to be rid of her. These goals should actually bring satisfaction to our physical, psychological and spiritual needs. If this is not the case in your life, then you need to weed out some useless activities.

Covetousness

THE PROBLEM

Covetousness is closely related to thorns, but slightly different. The problem of thorns views the effect of worries about external earthly matters. Covetousness views an attitude inside the person himself that leads to wrong activities.

The Greek word is a compound: *phileō* (to love), and *arguros* (silver). Thus we have *philarguria*—(the love of silver or money; avarice; covetousness). When money becomes so important to a man that the desire to accumulate more and more affects his happiness and influences his goals and moral principles, money becomes an end instead of merely a means, An excessive desire for money leads to unhappiness for many people who, instead of enjoying what they have, are chronically dissatisfied about what they do not have.

The Bible gives a clear warning against covetousness. The general effect of covetousness in non-Christians is described in I Timothy 6:9: "Those who purpose to be rich fall into temptation, into a trap and into many foolish and hurtful cravings" (expanded translation). Paul goes on to say that these cravings are of such a nature that they drown men into (bodily) destruction (*olethros*, loss of physical life in this world) and perdition (*apōleia*, eternal ruin and punishment in the next world; that is, eternal hell fire). The cravings that develop from covetousness lead men away from God. Men tend to become more and more enslaved by money and the things it can buy. A good example is the rich man, mentioned by Christ in Luke 16:19-26, who lived well in this life and failed to get ready for the next life, ending up in torment in hell.

The mental unhappiness that results from unsatisfied cravings is obvious. Covetousness leads to the development of many abnormal cravings for possessions, and when these desires are denied, depression results.

In I Timothy 6:10 Paul says that covetousness is a root of all kinds of evil (such as lying, stealing, murder, etc.). He points out that some Christians who have become too concerned with acquiring money have been led astray from the faith and have pierced themselves through with many sorrows (literally, consuming griefs). Such sorrows would include the dissatisfaction of excessive craving for material things, plus the guilt resulting from the violation of a moral principle.

THE REMEDY

Paul's remedy is both positive and negative: (1) Be fleeing the wrong things, such as covetousness; (2) Be pursuing the right things instead (I Tim. 6:11). In other words, the Christian must be on guard against letting himself become too interested in money. Once covetousness has developed it is hard to get rid of. The cure usually involves testing, such as a financial loss with its associated emotional suffering, in which the offensive craving for money is denied satisfaction.

Tendency to Avoid Facing Reality

THE PROBLEM

One human tendency that is very common is reluctance to face up to an unpleasant reality in life. For example, an unloved wife may refuse to admit to herself that her husband has lost interest in her, since this would be painful to face. She may prefer to pretend that no marital problem exists.

This tendency is unhealthy for several reasons. First, it fails to achieve any useful purpose and may result in mental disorder if the associated emotions are repressed. The unloved wife in this example still feels anxious and unhappy even though it may be on a subconscious level. Subconscious anxiety and unhappiness is just as real as conscious. On a conscious level this wife might feel chronically depressed but be confused as to the reason. She would have to face her problem on a conscious level in order to solve it and perhaps achieve happiness.

This second point, failure to recognize and face the problem, prevents anything from being done to correct the situation. A problem has to be recognized before it can be solved. Problems tend to gradually get worse over the years. So the longer one waits before trying to solve a problem, the harder it may become.

Third, this approach of avoiding reality is contrary to the Bible, in that it is inconsistent with the truth. For a husband and wife to pretend that they have no marital problem when one exists is to put forth a lie, which is an abomination to God (Prov. 12:22). Christians are told to think the truth (Phil. 4:8) and speak the truth (Eph. 4:25).

THE REMEDY

The only remedy is to face up to the truth, however unpleasant it may be. When we do this we may experience some unhappiness and anxiety initially. Sometimes the act of recognizing an unpleasant truth may be so upsetting that the counselor must give much support (and often tranquilizing medication) to the person involved. By support I mean emotional and spiritual encouragement and help from his friends, pastor, and doctor. If the anxiety is very great the person should consult a competent psychiatrist who can guide him through the problem so as to prevent a nervous breakdown.

Occasionally one finds a Christian who persists in denying the truth in spite of repeated confrontation with the facts. Although there may be several explanations for this, three should be noted especially. Often the person is rigid and dogmatic about everything. He avoids facing reality because it would require a change in his beliefs and thus an admission that he had been wrong about something in the past. This is hard for him to do. His stubbornness may prevent any progress.

Another is the person who avoids facing reality because it would necessitate his giving up something he wants in life, or perhaps accepting something he does not want. Such a person is actually in rebellion against God. Not having yielded his life to God, he is not willing to accept the circumstances God might send into his life.

A third is the emotionally disturbed person. He perceives, at least subconsciously, that to face on a conscious level an unpleasant truth may arouse enough anxiety to precipitate a nervous breakdown. Such a person is psychologically unable to face the unpleasant reality without psychiatric help. He uses the defense mechanism of denial to avoid a breakdown.

The problem of facing reality is not always a simple matter, but it is a goal we should all aim for.

Tendency to Avoid Accepting Responsibility

THE PROBLEM

This is closely related to the previous need to face reality, but it views the problem from a different angle. The person who avoids facing reality does not consciously perceive the truth, or only partly sees it. On the other hand, the person who avoids responsibility sees what he should do, but does not do it. The Bible mentions this principle in respect to how we show our Christian love (I John 3:18). We are to show it not only by what we think and say, but also by what we do.

This principle may affect mental health in several ways. First, privilege and responsibility always go together. It is unnatural to try to separate the two. The person who wants to play but never works (in order to earn the money and time for leisure recreation) will eventually be caught up short by the responsibilities which have been neglected. For instance, if he has not made the payments on his car, then eventually the car will be forcibly taken away from him. Also, the person who tries to work all the time and neglects his personal needs for relaxation and recreation will get into trouble. He will become nervous and tense from overwork. He is being irresponsible about his health.

Moreover, we often miss out on good things in life because we fail to take on the responsibility they require. A good example is friendship. Many people suffer from unhappiness because they lack friends. But to have friends we must reach out to other people with friendly overtures (Prov. 18:24). If we do not reach out in a friendly way then people are unlikely to respond in a friendly manner. Another example is the wife who loses the respect and love of her husband because she has not accepted the responsibilities of being a good wife and giving love.

I have listed this as a spiritual principle because the Bible recommends that we be *sober* (Rom. 12:3; I Tim. 3:2; Titus 2:12; I Peter 1:13). The word for sober here is *sōphrōn*. It means "sound minded," or we might say, having good common sense. This is another way of saying we should face reality and do the appropriate, responsible thing. Titus 2:12 gives us a good summary of how we should live in the present age: (1) *soberly;* this refers to being responsible and doing the right thing—that which is logically sound and sensible. (2) *righteously;* this means doing the right thing in relation to men—that which is morally right. (3) *godly;* this refers to doing the right thing in relation to God, thinking and behaving in a godly manner. This principle recognizes the demands of common sense, of justice, and of God in our lives.

So to try to live in a way contrary to logic or true common sense is to be irresponsible. This is easily seen in the realm of finance whenever a person tries to maintain a standard of living that is too high for his income. This is unrealistic and illogical, and therefore irresponsible.

THE REMEDY

The remedy, of course, is to accept our responsibilities. Ideally, a child is trained to do this in his early years if his parents are consistent and reasonable in their demands and discipline (Prov. 22:6). A child should be given enough, but not too much, responsibility during childhood. An error in either direction may make him reluctant to accept responsibility in adult life. If he reaches adult life still irresponsible, then only the hard knocks of everyday life, with God's help, and sometimes only with psychiatric help, can bring about improvement. Some people learn by experience, while others do not. It is distressing to see young people repeatedly get into trouble (such as writing bad checks), when the parents persist in bailing them out every time. As long as the irresponsible person can get away with his behavior without having to suffer the consequences, then he will continue to be irresponsible. We must accept responsibility to avoid the distressing loss of privileges which inevitably follows irresponsibility.

Satanic Attack

DEMON POSSESSION

Without a doubt Satan, usually working through his angels— demons or evil spirits under his authority—frequently has a hand in the development of mental trouble in Christians. This is substantiated by the biblical account of Christ's casting out of devils (Matt. 12:24-28).

I am not referring particularly to demon possession, although I am assured by some missionaries who have observed such cases on the mission field that demon possession in Christians does occur, resulting in abnormal mental or physical behavior. And the Bible indicates that demon possession can be expressed by a mental disorder in a person who is not a Christian (see Luke 8:27, 29, 35). However, I believe that Satan more often attacks Christians in ways other than demon possession. Before I discuss these other ways, I believe a few words should be said concerning demon possession in Christians. Some people claim that since the body of a Christian is indwelt by God the Holy Spirit, that both the Holy Spirit and the demon could not control the same body. Some say that it is impossible for both the Holy Spirit and a demon to indwell the same body. But there is no direct proof that both the Holy Spirit and a demon could not dwell in the same body. The one who says it cannot happen must bear the burden of proving that it cannot happen, using Scripture properly interpreted and applied. This is difficult in the face of the numerous reports of people who seem to be real Christians and who apparently have suffered from demon possession.

Second, how do we know that the demon possesses the Christian? In such a case it is very doubtful that the body of the Christian is possessed by the demon. What does happen? Well, nobody knows exactly what happens. It seems that at times the demon is able to gain enough influence over the mind and body of the Christian who suffers from a demon so that the demon can manifest itself in the form of the unusual and frequently evil symptoms of mind and body, perhaps seizures and/or mental derangements. Actually, the word *influence* is more accurate than the word *possess*. A Christian's mind might become strongly influenced by a demon, causing spells, but in between these fits of demoniac behavior the Christian may be perfectly normal. This off-and-on character may distinguish demon possession from true psychotic mental disease, which leaves the person mentally disordered most of the time. So a demon may exert a strong influence over a Christian even though his body is indwelt by the Holy Spirit.

Moreover, just because a Christian's body is indwelt by the Holy Spirit, this does not necessarily mean that this particular

Christian is *controlled* by the Holy Spirit. In fact he may be living in open rebellion against God, resisting the promptings of the Holy Spirit. There seems to be no reason why such a Christian cannot be exploited and used by a demon in a bizarre, peculiar manner such as so-called "demon possession." This is really not very different from the other ways in which demons deceive, mislead and influence Christians (see Mark 8:33; Acts 5:3).

In regard to the possibility of ordinary mental disease, as we see it today, being a form of demon-possession, I have no doubt that it is possible. It may have happened before, but I frankly do not know how one could recognize and distinguish such cases and differentiate them from ordinary insanity. A demon could very well be behind the mental symptoms seen in mental illness. But how could we prove that the demon is causing these symptoms?

Although demons may affect mental illness, I believe that most cases of mental disease in Christians are the result of a combination of the many factors which are discussed in this study. Satan and his demons are most active in urging Christians to continue practicing poor habits which lead to mental breakdowns. This is such a fruitful field for demon influence that such an extreme form of attack as demon possession is not usually necessary.

Satan is more likely to attack a Christian who is psychologically or physically weakened than one who is healthy in these areas. Satan uses lies and deceptions, which, when added to other external pressures, can combine to cause a breakdown. Satan may attack a Christian who is suffering from psychological distress and try to tear him down spiritually. The Christian needs to become acquainted with the different ways in which Satan works so that he can learn how to defend himself.

The clearest Bible verse which establishes the fact of Satan's activity in regard to attacking Christians is II Corinthians 12:7 where Paul says that "there was given to me a thorn in the flesh," which Paul explains as "the messenger of Satan to buffet me." We do not know what the thorn was, but we do know that it produced a permanent problem, leaving him with an infirmity (weakness, see II Cor. 12:9). God would not remove this problem, but He gave Paul special grace to withstand it.

But what would have happened if Paul had been physically fatigued when this hit him, or ignorant that Satan had a hand in it, or too tired to pray about it, or rebellious toward God with unconfessed sin? Such a condition would have prevented him from having a close spiritual relationship with God. Had Paul been a Christian with poor spiritual habits, had he been ignorant of the Word of God which teaches that God will give grace to help in time of need if we come to Him (Heb. 4:16), what then? If Paul had been in this condition, then he might have had a nervous breakdown.

Even the Apostle Paul, in his fine spiritual condition, admitted that this thorn in the flesh weakened him. He was buffeted by it, tossed around somewhat like a ship is buffeted by a storm at sea. But Paul accepted it as God's will and realized that it (1) kept him from being proud (II Cor. 12:7), and (2) made him stronger spiritually by making him more consciously dependent upon God (v. 10).

We do not know what lies the demon suggested to Paul when he suffered from this infirmity; but we can imagine, because Satan is a liar (John 8:44) and a deceiver (Rev. 12:9), that he may have repeatedly whispered disturbing lies to Paul. Perhaps he said: "Paul, this time next year this condition will be so bad you won't be able to preach any more." Or, "Paul, you have to drop all this evangelism and Bible study and go seek a better doctor who can cure you. Do it now, or it will be too late. The advice of your doctor friend Luke is not trustworthy." Or, "Paul, this thing will affect your mind, you know. It can leave you permanently insane. There is no cure for it."

If Paul had not known what to do about the lies of Satan, he could have been overwhelmed with discouragement and depression. Using the weapons and methods available to a Christian, Paul struggled with the problem, continuing in prayer (II Cor. 12:8) until the Lord would either (1) take away the problem or (2) give grace to endure the effects of it. God did the latter (v. 9).

We need to become familiar with the different ways in which Satan works, so that we can be on guard against him. We should not be ignorant of his devices (II Cor. 2:11). We need to learn how God expects us to fight off Satan and how much we can expect God to do.

Satan's Methods

Let us see from the Bible the many different ways in which Satan works. He wages a constant warfare against Christians (Eph. 6:12). We must be aware of a twofold problem concerning satanic attack. One is the difficulty in recognizing Satan's attack, since a thought planted in the mind by Satan will seem the same as any other spontaneous thought. We must learn something of Satan's methods so that we can counteract his deception.

A second factor is that Satan discovers our weak points and tries to attack us in our most vulnerable areas. This brings us immediately to the factor of psychological problems. A psychological problem is definitely a weak point which Satan would try to aggravate. Paul warns in I Corinthians 7:5 that a married couple should have uninterrupted sexual relations, since the lack of sexual satisfaction would produce frustration. A person thus robbed of his normal sexual outlet often becomes vulnerable to temptation. And Satan might exploit such a condition, hoping to induce the Christian to commit a sexually immoral act. Obviously the resolution of psychological problems leads to less vulnerability to an attack from Satan, and more self-control.

Without a doubt Satan can be instrumental in precipitating physical illness, which always causes emotional, physical and spiritual strain. This fact is well substantiated in the Bible (see Matt. 9:32-33; 12:22; 17:15, 18; Luke 8:36; Job 2:7). This is another way in which Satan acts to put the pressure on a Christian.

Some doctors feel that the idea of satanic attack in physical illness is contrary to the findings of medical science, but that is not so. Medical science has demonstrated that infectious diseases, for instance, are caused by germs, such as bacteria. However, why a particular person, at a particular moment, will become infected and sick from a certain germ, while people all around him do not, cannot be explained by medical science. Medical science explains the how of sickness, but it does not always know the why. A certain sickness may be caused by a germ, but Satan can work through the laws of nature governing infections in such a way that certain persons will become sick at his will. The laws of nature that are known today are not the only laws that are operating. In addition there are certain supernatural laws about which we know very little.

Why would Satan make a Christian sick? There are several reasons. In II Corinthians 12:9 it is implied that sickness produces weakness. A sick person does not have the emotional and spiritual stamina of a healthy person and he may break down sooner under mental pressure. And when a person is sick he is likely to become careless about his spiritual habits. Satan hopes to make him so burdened that he will either break down or at least be spiritually weakened.

Satan acts in ways that put pressure on men. The word "vex" in Luke 6:18 and Acts 5:16 means literally "to crowd or harass." Also the word "oppress" in Acts 10:38 means literally "to overpower."

Another way that Satan acts against Christians is to make non-Christians hostile to them, to stir them up to oppose the Christians. We know from scriptures like Ephesians 2:2 and II Timothy 2:26 that Satan dominates the minds of unsaved men and uses them to carry out his purposes upon the earth. (See also John 13:2; Acts 13:8-10.) Satan tries to make life hard for Christians. He may move the heart of a non-Christian boss to dislike a Christian employee, and as a result the Christian employee may have a hard time at work or may lose his job. Sometimes Satan will even use another Christian as a stumbling block (see Matt. 16:22-23; Mark 8:33).

One thing to keep in mind is that Satan does not want the Christian to be aware of his activity. He prefers to constantly feed the Christian disturbing thoughts that do not appear to be satanic lies. These lies will be ineffective only if the Christian meets them with faith and Scripture.

However, some Christians have trouble believing I John 1:9, which says that when you confess to (that is, agree with) God about your sin, then He forgives you. Satan comes along and says, "But this sin is different. It is worse than the others—it is so bad that God cannot forgive you. And besides, you have done it more than once. You will never have fellowship with God again."

This is a lie to prevent the Christian from having peace of mind through forgiveness of sin. The only remedy is for the Christian to believe by faith what God has said in I John 1:9, and take his stand on the scriptures against Satan. James 4:7 urges the Christian to take a stand against (resist) Satan, and adds that when a Christian does this, Satan flees. How does one take a stand against Satan? First of all, he must have something upon which to stand. And the only trustworthy ground to stand upon is the truth of God's Word, properly applied to the situation.

Since God has said that He will forgive sins, the Christian must stand on that promise and tell Satan he is a liar. His faith in God's promise will shield him from the damaging, disturbing effect of Satan's fiery dart. This shield will protect him from the depression and discouragement that such a lie could produce.

Notice that the main weapon against Satan is defensive. It is *faith*, resting in the Word of God, which acts as a shield (Eph. 6:16). When Christ was attacked by Satan in the wilderness He quoted the scriptures to him and Satan left Him (Matt. 4:4-11). Satan often tempts Christians to commit sinful acts (Acts 5:3; I Cor. 7:5), and puts evil thoughts into their minds. These thoughts should be put out immediately.

Satan also frequently sets a trap (I Tim. 3:7) in order to turn Christians aside into error (I Tim. 5:15), just as he tried to cause Christ to stumble (Matt. 16:23). He looks for an occasion to revile us (I Tim. 5:14) and accuse us of sin (Rev. 12:10). The word "devil" means "slanderer," and Satan tries to slander us at every opportunity.

Satan's aim with Christians is to get them to do that which is contrary to God's Word and to prevent them from obeying God. In order to promote his plan he tries to deceive the Christian as to what is the truth. Satan promotes a system of error (Eph. 6:11; I Tim. 4:1). He has workers, false teachers, teaching lies (II Cor. 11:13-15).

If he can deceive us concerning the truth about God, then he can corrupt our minds (II Cor. 11:3). He will try to make us doubt God's Word, as he made Eve do (Gen. 3:1). A knowledge and an understanding of the truth of the Bible is essential to keep us from being deceived and led astray. Satan calls evil good, and he calls good evil. He confuses moral issues which we must keep straight. A Christian who is confused about what is right and wrong is heading for trouble. Satan can lead him astray into sin that will damage his soul.

In answer to the question "Why would God permit Satan to attack the Christian?" I answer that God does not permit anything to happen to us that is not designed to work out for our good (Rom. 8:28). Satan may be used by God to discipline disobedient Christians (I Cor. 5:5; I Tim. 1:20). Or God may permit Satan to test an obedient Christian so that he may realize the presence of a spiritual defect or weakness of which he was unaware, as in the case of Peter (Luke 22:31). Peter was overconfident, with a tendency to trust in his own ability. He had to fail before he could learn that he must depend upon God.

The Remedy for Satanic Attack

I have already mentioned the need to resolve psychological problems, producing less vulnerability to satanic attack, as well as ways to fight off Satan and his demons. In I Peter 5:8-9 we find a three-point analysis of procedure in this warfare: (1) preparation for warfare, (2) attitude of mind in battle, and (3) actual warfare.

Preparation for warfare. Peter tells us (I Peter 5:8) to be sober. Warfare with Satan is serious business. Unless we are sober and serious about our Christianity we are not likely to take seriously the threat and danger of satanic attack. Being sober includes the concept of being psychologically healthy.

A soldier who is going to war is usually serious-minded since he knows he will have to fight and be exposed to attack. He will

manifest an intense interest in: (1) the weapons available for
use against the enemy, (2) the tactics and forces of the enemy,
(3) effective defense against the different types of attack the
enemy will use, and (4) the help he can expect from his com-
mander. He will desire good training. Likewise, as Christians
we need good training before we start thinking about entering
into battle with Satan. Unless we are serious and sober about
our Christianity, we may find it hard to be victorious over Satan.
Satan may fool us and defeat us.

The Christian who is sober will take the time and effort to
study God's Word to become familiar with the ways in which
Satan works. He will prepare for warfare by becoming familiar
with the weapons which God has provided and by learning ex-
perientially how to walk with God.

What are our weapons for this warfare? We do not war according to the flesh (II Cor. 10:3), and the weapons of our warfare "are not fleshly, but are mighty" (v. 4) from the viewpoint of
God. Their use results in the "pulling down of strong holds."
Ephesians 6:11 points out that the weapons are of God and con-
stitute a suit of armor which will protect us when we take a
stand against the devil.

The same exhortation for taking a stand against Satan is found
in Ephesians 6:13, and is the third point in this analysis. The
Christian should "take up" (Eph. 6:13) and "put on" (v. 11) all
the armor and weapons of Ephesians 6:14-17, even before he
leaves basic training camp. After he has done this he is ready
to go out to the battlefield. We also need to know that in this
battle God Himself (Exodus 14:14, 25; Joshua 23:3, 9-10; I Sam.
17:37, 45-47; II Chron. 20:15, 17) and His angels (II Kings 6:15-
17; Dan. 6:22) fight for us.

We must be willing to endure the hardships of being a soldier
(Heb. 10:32), which may involve suffering (I Peter 1:6; 5:10).
Paul reminded Timothy of this in II Timothy 2:3. The Christian
who will be an effective soldier against Satan may not always
be able to live luxuriously. Sometimes he may have to endure
inconveniences in order to remain spiritually strong and to stand
fast against Satan. Satan sometimes tries to lure Christians into

traps, using as bait many of the luxuries and pleasures of this world.

Having become educated and trained as to our weapons and our enemy, and then having put on our armor and taken up our weapons, we are ready to go forth to the battlefield. Where is the battlefield for the Christian? It is any place of obedience or service. Notice that immediately after Christ's baptism, an act of obedience, the devil met Him and tempted Him. The moment a Christian makes up his mind that he is going to live a life of obedience to the Lord, that he is going to do what the Lord commands and go where the Lord directs, then he is on the Christian battlefield and Satan begins working against him.

Attitude of mind in battle. The next thing Peter tells us to do (I Peter 5:8) is to be vigilant. This word means "awake and watchful." A soldier on duty on the battlefield cannot go to sleep or the enemy will approach him and launch an attack. Satan is like a lion walking about trying to maneuver himself into a favorable position from which to attack us. We must be on guard against this and we must not give the adversary even one favorable opportunity for reviling (I Tim. 5:14). The word for "opportunity" here is a military word that refers to a "base of operations from which to launch an attack." Avoid letting Satan get you into a position where you are vulnerable to attack, where he can throw a fiery dart at you. Ephesians 4:27 says, "Stop giving an opportunity for action [literally, a place] to the devil." This will enable you to avoid a certain amount of unnecessary warfare with the devil.

Christ had this in mind in the Garden of Gethsemane when He said, "Watch and pray, lest you enter into temptation." The disciples did not watch and they did not pray. Instead they went to sleep and soon found themselves in the midst of a big temptation. They were tempted to turn coward and run when Christ was arrested instead of standing fast as loyal disciples. They failed because they were not prepared for the trial. If they had listened to Christ when He told them it was necessary for the Messiah to die on the cross, they would have known what to expect. They would have been prepared for the crisis and perhaps could have avoided an unnecessary clash with the soldiers who arrested Christ. They would have been watchful and might have avoided this needless encounter with the forces of evil and been more courageous and steadfast in their testimony.

We should notice, while we are discussing our attitude on the battlefield, that Christ couples together "watch and pray." Paul does the same thing in Ephesians 6:18 where he exhorts us to be constantly "praying" and "watching with perseverance and supplication." As we watch, vigilant, on the lookout for the enemy, we should constantly pray that God will enable us to avoid unnecessary conflicts with Satan and keep us out of situations which give Satan an advantage over us.

However, we will not be able to completely avoid contact with the enemy. He will continue to attack, especially when God is using us in a ministry which threatens Satan's control of unsaved men, such as at an evangelistic meeting. He also seems to attack especially at times when we are weakened from other causes, such as a physical illness. We should be on guard against him especially during those times.

This bring us to the third phase of our procedure in this warfare, the actual battle.

The actual warfare. The first thing we must realize is that we do not fight merely with our natural ability (II Cor. 10:3), but in the energy of the Spirit. Fighting Satan is part of our walk, and we must walk by the Spirit. In Ephesians 6:10 Paul says to "keep on being strengthened by the Lord and the manifested power of His inherent strength," and, in Ephesians 3:16, he prays that they might be "strengthened through the agency of His Spirit in regard to the inward man." We can expect God to strengthen us with power for this battle if we are trusting Him to do so. How can we be sure that God will strengthen us in this struggle? Philippians 2:13 clearly says that God keeps on "working" (literally, energizing) in us so that we will be willing to do that which is "in behalf of [His] good pleasure." Literally, the verse says, "God energizes us to want to do and to be energetic to do that which pleases Him."

When the Christian purposes to please God, then the Lord will strengthen him to do it. Colossians 1:11 says that the Christian is constantly "being empowered with every power [literally, ability] . . . unto all patient endurance and all longsuffering with joy." In Colossians 1:29 Paul says that he is "laboring and engaging in combat according to His [i.e., God's] operative power [literally, with ability]." While Paul was laboring, God was constantly energizing him with ability. Upon such verses as these we can take our stand, and trust in God to energize us to struggle in this conflict. God will not energize us to do that which is contrary to His will. When the Christian attempts to fight in the energy of the flesh, he finds it too hard and gives up. Without God's power his efforts are useless.

We are to take up a stand against Satan just as a soldier in battle takes up a certain position and determines to hold it and not fall back. Likewise we are to take up a battle position against Satan and not give way. This involves the use of these weapons: (1) faith, used as a shield (Eph. 6:16); (2) the spoken (or quoted) Word of God, used as a sword (v. 17). Our faith has to rest upon something concrete, and we need the Word of God, committed to memory, as our basis of faith.

We need the shield and the sword during Satan's attack to take our stand against him. The Greek word for "taking a stand against" occurs in I Peter 5:8; James 4:7; and Ephesians 6:13. In actual warfare a soldier who is being attacked by the enemy takes up a battle position and fights to hold that position. And, similarly, our warfare with Satan is primarily defensive. We are not told to attempt to engage in any offensive warfare against Satan. The sword of the Word is not for offensive attack, but for the purpose of driving Satan back so that we can hold our position. James 4:7 says, "Take a stand against the devil, and he will flee from you." It does not say, "Then leave your position and start chasing Satan and launch a counterattack." At the present time this world system is under the control of Satan, and this makes the Christian a stranger in a hostile world. God has not ordered us to conquer the world, but to be a testimony to the truth and to announce the gospel to the world. God Himself will conquer the world at the proper time. To try to attack Satan offensively is foolish and is contrary to scriptural teaching. Even Michael, the archangel, when contending with the devil about the body of Moses "did not dare to bring against [the devil] a judgment of slander," but instead said, "May the Lord rebuke you" (Jude 9).

Now it is true that God sometimes sends missionaries into areas where Satan's false religions dominate. In a sense this is an offensive attack. But keep in mind that it is God who is doing the attacking. He is merely using the Christian as the instrument to carry the gospel. Behind the scenes God and a mighty army of angels are doing the actual offensive warfare. The Lord alone can offensively attack Satan. So the emphasis of Scripture is that as Christians we are to be on the defensive. We are not told to "rush forward courageously in attack"; rather we are told to "take up a battle position," and, after having taken our stand, we are to "remain steadfast" (Eph. 6:13).

Let me illustrate how one takes a stand against Satan. Suppose a Christian has made arrangements to go to Africa as a missionary and he has only a few days left to buy his ticket for the trip. He knows that if God really wants him to go He will see to it that he receives the money to buy the ticket. How can he be sure of this? His assurance comes from a verse like Philippians 4:19: "My God shall supply every need of yours according to His riches in glory in Christ Jesus." If passage to Africa is really a need *in God's estimation*, then He will supply the need. While he is waiting for the money to come in, this Christian takes his stand and rests upon this verse. He may not have the money yet, but if God wants him on that ship, he does not have to be anxious about it. He can have peace of mind knowing that God will supply the need.

Along comes Satan, who wants to take away his peace and make him worried and anxious. How does he attack him? He lies, "But you probably won't get the money in time. Remember the people back in your home church who promised to give you the money? Well, they didn't send it, did they? You cannot depend on Christians. They will let you down every time. Now it is too late for anyone back at your church to know about your need; besides, you don't feel free to call back and beg someone to send you money. The boat is going to leave without you. Nobody knows about your need and nobody cares. There is no hope." What a fiery dart!

How can the Christian avoid becoming depressed and discouraged? He can see no solution in sight, but he does not walk by sight. He walks by faith. He takes his stand upon the promise of God and lets God solve the problem in His own way and in His own time.

If the money does not come in and the boat sails without him, then the Christian's only proper conclusion can be that the Lord's will did not actually include his getting on that boat. God wanted him to go as far as he did, but at that particular point He stopped him. He must be confident that God will reveal a new plan to him at the proper time. Perhaps the Lord was testing his willingness to go to Africa, and when he proved he was willing, then God kept him from going because He wanted to use him in a different place. If Christ is the Lord of his life, then the Lord has the right to send the Christian to any place.

Let us take a hypothetical case of a Christian woman who has experienced a nervous breakdown from a combination of factors: a chronic state of fatigue from several years of overwork without a vacation; a physical illness that left her weakened still further; some sins in her life which she has not handled properly, never really agreeing with God about them; and a severe emotional trial precipitated by the death of a person very close to her. Following the death of her loved one, terrible feelings of utter exhaustion, weakness, lack of interest and depression come and boil up into despair and anxiety. She is so weak that she cannot do her housework and has to stay in bed much of the time. Realizing her mistake, she becomes sober and serious. She realizes that there are several things in her life that are not right which she has known about for some time but has done nothing about. She prays to God confessing her sins and begins straightening out her life. The Lord forgives her, and if she again fails and sins in one of these ways, He will forgive her again and will cleanse her and protect her from further damage from this sin. Of course in previous years these sins were not confessed when they were committed. This resulted in damage to her soul which contributed to her illness. A damaged soul cannot behave properly and cannot experience good mental health. The effects of this damage will have to run their course.

Does she improve immediately after confessing these sins? Perhaps not. Although confession prevents any further hurt, it does not remove the damage to her mind and soul done in previous years. She may not improve very much until the reaping process has run its course. She has sown a crop of sins; now she will have to reap them. It is unlikely that she can experience strong peace of mind during this reaping process. Recovery takes time. However, she can be encouraged that things will get better in time. When she accepts this, she can be less impatient and frustrated.

What is Satan doing during this time? In the first place he has probably put pressure on her that exaggerated the emotional strain experienced in the death of her loved one. Satan attacked her right after this storm of life came, and she was unprepared to cope with him. Now he keeps up the pressure on her in several ways. He is constantly feeding her lies: "You have lost your mind and you will never be sane again." Or, "What a hardship this is upon your family! You ought to be ashamed to be acting this way." Or, "They have stopped loving you because you are so sickly."

Satan may bombard her with a variety of physical symptoms, such as a "fluttering of the heart," or "headaches," or "weakness," or "nervous feelings." When she feels her heart flutter then Satan lies to her, "Say, you must be getting a heart attack." Satan tries to make her panic. If the doctor is able to convince her that her heart is in good shape, then Satan may bring on a different symptom and more lies.

What can she do about these disturbing symptoms and depressing thoughts? Regarding the thoughts, if she is going to avoid panic, she will have to become aware that Satan may be

oppressing her. Then she can take a stand upon the truth of the
Word of God, claiming verses such as I Peter 5:10, which assures
her that after she has suffered awhile, God will repair and establish her again. She can form the habit of thinking upon things that
are true (Phil. 4:8) instead of brooding over the lies of Satan.
Then Satan's fiery darts will become less effective. She can also
begin correcting the psychological problems she has. She can try
to learn from her mistakes.

But what can she do about physical symptoms? Of course not
all are caused by Satan, and some may be easily relieved by
medicine. There is nothing wrong with relieving the physical
symptoms if possible, since God has provided these remedies by
revealing to medical science the knowledge about them. To a
person who cannot sleep at night a sleeping pill is a real blessing
from God. The physical symptoms which cannot be relieved she
must simply endure. Hebrews 10:32, and 11:34, 37 show that
sometimes God's will for the life of the Christian includes physical suffering. This Christian woman can endure the symptoms
which cannot be relieved by reminding herself that they are permitted by God, and that God will give her grace to endure them.
She can discipline herself to stop measuring her progress by her
physical feelings, and even to ignore her physical feelings to a
certain extent. She can learn to measure her condition by faith,
confident in her understanding of what has happened to her, if
she trusts in the Lord for help.

No matter what the problem is, whether the lies of Satan or
physical illness, a Christian can have some peace of mind if he
will leave the problem in God's hands and rest confidently in
God's promises. There may not always be complete peace of
mind, but there will be at least a feeling of reassurance and hope.
God does guard our hearts and minds with His peace, but only
when we truly trust Him to help us cope with our problems.

CHAPTER TEN

CAUSES OF CHRISTIAN IMMATURITY

The Meaning of Christian Immaturity

CHRISTIAN IMMATURITY refers to lack of growth as a Christian. In the physical realm a child who grows older in years but does not mature physically is recognized as abnormal. If you had a child who was not growing and gaining in weight you would take him to the doctor and say, "Something is wrong."

Something is also wrong when a Christian fails to steadily develop and grow spiritually. I Peter 2:2 tells us as Christians to have an "eager longing for the unadulterated milk of the Word" in order that we may "grow by means of it" and "make progress in [our] salvation." This does not mean to become more saved, but it means to become in thinking and behavior more like a saved person. In Hebrews 5:13-14 a clear distinction is made between spiritually immature Christians, referred to as "unskillful [literally, inexperienced] in a word [or matter] of righteousness" (v. 13), and mature Christians who, "by reason of use [literally, because of practice], have their senses [that is, powers of perception] exercised to discern [literally, for distinguishing between] both good and evil" (v. 14). Here it is emphasized that the man of full spiritual age (literally, the mature one) is able to distinguish between good and evil and thus is more efficient in discerning the Lord's will.

The word here for maturity (translated in the King James Version as "of full age") is *teleios*, which implies completeness. When applied to the concept of maturity it means "full-grown" or "mature." This same word, *teleios*, is used by Paul in Ephesians 4:13 where he says that one of the purposes of the ministry gifts is that the Christian might become a "perfect man" (literally, a mature man), meaning spiritually mature. In verse 14 Paul goes on to say that the maturity is needed "in order that we may no longer be infants, tossed to and fro and whirled around in circles by every wind of teaching by the trickery of men, [this trickery being accomplished] by a cunning craftiness which has as its purpose the furthering of the scheming, deceitful system which is characterized by a wandering astray [from the truth]" (literal, expanded translation). In other words, we need to be spiritually mature to have the proper judgment and discernment so as to avoid being misled by a false theological system inspired by Satan. Satan would like us to be misled as to what is the truth, and we will be misled unless we are spiritually mature.

This same idea is the subject of Paul's prayer for the Colossian Christians (Col. 1:9). Here he prays that they might be filled (that is, become complete or fully developed) with the full knowledge of His (God's) will in the realm of every (kind of) wisdom and discernment. The word for "fill" here is *plēroō*, which means "to fill" or "to complete." The Christian's mind is to be pervaded throughout by the knowledge of God's will.

But, what exactly is spiritual maturity? It resembles ordinary psychological maturity. It is a giving up of the old way of thinking and a taking on of more mature ways of thinking and behaving (that is, more proper for a Christian). When one first becomes a Christian he has some wisdom, but part of it is the "wisdom of the world." The world's wisdom is any philosophy or set of beliefs which is contrary to the truth of God. Paul says that the "wisdom of this world is foolishness [literally, stupidity] from the viewpoint of God" (I Cor. 3:19). To put it simply, we have to learn a new philosophy, or way of thinking, which Paul calls "God's wisdom" (I Cor. 2:7). Paul says that there is a "wisdom we speak among the mature ones [again *teleios*], but it is not a wisdom known by the ordinary (non-Christian) person in this age" (I Cor. 2:6, 8).

Growing up as a Christian involves getting rid of the old bad spiritual habits and establishing new and better spiritual habits. We read in God's Word what habits we should acquire and what habits we should get rid of. We ought to set as our goal obedience to these instructions. We are to form good habits such as: prayer to God; study and meditation upon God's Word; obedience to God's laws; trusting in God instead of in money, power, or people. We are to get rid of such habits as lying, cheating, stealing, slandering, and cursing. If we do not make any progress, if we do not steadily become better Christians, then we may be going in the other direction. A swimmer who is not swimming upstream is usually drifting downstream. Too many Christians are drifters. They seem to get along well, not really concerned about the matter of Christian growth. They continue their old ways of living until something upsetting happens. It may be a severe trial or test which they are utterly unprepared to handle, and it may break them. It takes a mature Christian, one with good spiritual habits, to weather a severe storm of life. When our way of thinking has changed so that it closely corresponds to God's way of thinking, to God's wisdom, and when our habits have changed in a corresponding manner, then we are spiritually mature.

Development of Christian Maturity

How do we acquire this new way of thinking and behaving? How is the old way of thinking dethroned? The Bible reveals several things about this process. First, this learning process is carried on by the teaching ministry of God the Holy Spirit. Christ said the Spirit would teach Christians when He came (John 16:13-14). John also emphasized that the Holy Spirit is our teacher (I John 2:27), although He may utilize human instruments as tools for teaching, to whom He gives gifts of teaching ability (Eph. 4:11). The things taught by the Spirit (that is, God's wisdom) seem foolish to a non-Christian man because they can be understood only by the aid of the Holy Spirit (I Cor. 2:12-14).

Second, we come to really understand and use this new wisdom by applying it in our daily life experiences, especially in testing (Heb. 5:14; 12:7, 11). James urges us to count it all joy when we

fall into testing (James 1:2). He adds that the aim of testing is
to produce patience (patient endurance) (v. 3). The resulting
patience is to carry out its work in us in order that we may be mature (here again, *teleios*) and intact, lacking in nothing (v. 4).
The experience of testing demands that we put to use our new
wisdom. In this way it becomes part of our permanent spiritual
equipment. James goes on to say that if anyone lacks wisdom then
he should keep on praying to God who will give him the wisdom
he needs (v. 5).

Paul, in Philippians 3:15, reminds us that mature ones (*teleios*
again) are to be mature minded ("be thus minded" in King James
Version), and if anyone is thinking differently (that is, different
from maturely or wisely), then God will reveal this to him. Here
is God's promise that He will continue to make known to us our
immature ways of thinking. So by acquiring knowledge of the
truth in God's Word and by experiencing testing—practice at applying the knowledge—we can become wise and mature.

Causes of Persisting Immaturity

In general, there are three basic causes of persistent immaturity.

Bad Spiritual Habits. Notice in I Peter 2:1-2 that several things
must be done before we can have an eager longing for the Word
of God. The expression "put off" in verse 1 refers to getting rid of
a bad habit. Peter here says that before a Christian can have a
normal healthy appetite for God's Word, he must put off: (1)
malice (literally, bad-heartedness); (2) deceit; (3) hypocrisy;
(4) envy; and (5) slander. If a Christian is not willing to get rid
of these habits he will not be able to develop a good appetite for
God's Word. He must be willing to try, with God's help, to rid
himself of them before much progress can be made. Titus 2:12
tells us to "live soberly, righteously, and godly in this present
world." Paul also indicates that before we can do this we must
"deny ungodliness and worldly lusts." This is the prerequisite to
feeding on the Word and developing spiritually.

Thorns Which Choke the Word. Even a healthy plant with
plenty of food and water will not grow if it is choked by thorns
and weeds. Neither will the Christian grow and develop if he

allows the garden of his spiritual life to become overgrown with spiritual thorns which choke out the Word of God. There is competition between the Holy Spirit causing God's Word to take root in our lives and bear fruit, and the flesh, our old nature, which strives to prevent growth (Gal. 5:17). The old nature tends to lust after the luxuries, pleasures, money, power, and other things of this world in which it finds enjoyment. These things are not sinful in themselves. But the excessive or improper use of them is sin (I Cor. 7:31). The Christian can become so involved in them that he has no time or energy left for spiritual things. The Christian who invests all of his time, effort, and interest in secular things cannot expect the Word of God to have much influence upon his life. He cannot expect to reap great spiritual profit when he has made no spiritual investment.

In Mark 4:18-19 and Luke 8:14 Christ uses good seed planted in the ground to illustrate the Word of God which is planted in a man's heart. In this case He shows that the presence of thorns in the ground will hinder the growth of the seed and choke it off. The end result is that the Word of God does not produce fruit (Mark 4:19), and the Christian does not become spiritually mature or produce good works. These thorns are harmful and must be avoided, since they can hinder spiritual growth. The Bible gives three generals kinds of thorns.

1. "THE ANXIOUS CARES OF THE AGE" (Mark 4:19). This thorn is called the "anxious cares [worries] of life" in Luke 8:14. What does it refer to? In Luke the word of *life* is *bios* and refers to the ordinary necessities of everyday life. Christians may worry about paying monthly bills such as house rent, food, utilities, clothes, payments on a new car, furniture, appliances, television set, insurance, toys, vacations, recreation, medical and dental expenses, and other items which are part of everyday life.

Anything and everything has a way of coming to seem like a necessity. Today if you asked many Christians to name the necessities of life, they would probably give a long list of things, many of which would be luxuries. The Bible limits real necessities to two: food and clothes (I Tim. 6:8). We might think that a permanent place to sleep would be an additional necessity. But

Christ, when He started on His earthly ministry, did not have a permanent home. God the Father always saw to it that Christ found a temporary place to sleep. Of course it is not wrong to set up a permanent home. We may not always have the most expensive home, but it will be what God thinks is adequate. God has not promised to give the Christian every luxury available today. It is an error to assume that because a person has the money to buy a certain luxury, God wants him to have it. This may not be true at all. It may become a stumbling block to spiritual growth.

It is easy to see how a man can become burdened with monthly payments that take every penny of his paycheck. If he has to struggle to make all his payments, perhaps worrying about overdue bills while trying to figure out how he can buy a new car, this anxious concern over life's needs will act as a thorn. Worry over such things uses up much available mental energy. Instead of being occupied with the things of God, such a person tends to become preoccupied with the things of the world. God is gradually crowded out of his thoughts, and his spiritual condition gradually deteriorates.

So the Christian should ask himself a question whenever he is considering a large purchase. "Is the purchase and use of this going to put me under such a financial strain that I might become overly anxious about my bills?" If you can buy and use the item without an anxious preoccupation with it, you have passed the thorn test. For instance, if your income fluctuates, dropping in the summer so that you could not keep up payments on a new car, then perhaps it would be better to wait and buy it when you are more financially able. People often become worried about bills they owe because they have bought too much too fast. Christians should avoid getting into a situation that involves such financial pressure. We should be honest and objective about what is a necessity and what is a luxury and exercise logical restraint in spending money. For a Christian to be overly worried about luxuries, or even about the necessities of life, is sin. In Philippians 4:6 God commands us to stop being overly worried about anything. Instead we are to trust in God to help to solve the problem or to provide grace to live with it. To continue worrying may sometimes be related to a lack of belief in God's trustworthiness.

2. "DECEITFULNESS OF RICHES" (Mark 4:19). This thorn is called the "wealth of life" in Luke 8:14. The Bible clearly says that covetousness (literally, love for money) is a root of all kinds of evil (I Tim. 6:10). Men may commit many kinds of crime for the sake of money, such as robbery, assault, and murder. Sometimes loss of money results in serious mental depression. When we lust after more money than we need, we often become chronically frustrated and dissatisfied.

The pursuit of riches is a poor goal in itself. To a person under pressure, worrying about the "anxious cares of the age," more money may seem a blessing. But this is deceptive. Money does not bring happiness by itself. It tends to deceive us by making us think that we cannot get along without it. We must remember that money is only the means to an end, not an end in itself. To want to acquire a large sum of money in order to carry out a specific worthy goal may be acceptable. To provide our family with a comfortable and happy life is, of course, a reasonable goal. But just where do we draw the line as to what is reasonable or unnecessary? What is useful or extravagant?

A person's heart can be drawn aside from spiritual things by a preoccupation with money. Paul pointed out two pitfalls common to the wealthy: pride, and false trust in riches as security. Although riches are uncertain (I Tim. 6:17) and perishable (I Peter 1:18), people still tend to trust in them. When money occupies too much of a person's time, energy, and attention, it becomes sin.

You can tell where a person's heart is by looking at what kind of treasure he is building up (Luke 12:34). If his heart is on heavenly things (Col. 3:2) he will be building up heavenly treasure—investing his time and energy in spiritual things. If his heart is on earthly things, such as money, he will be more interested in earthly, secular activities.

We should consider the effect of money before making a decision about the Lord's will for our life. Would an opportunity to make a million dollars always be the Lord's will? Not necessarily. In fact, if success would produce preoccupation with the money it would not be the Lord's will. However, some are able to have wealth and remain unspoiled. Obtaining a large amount of money may be acceptable and within the Lord's will for them.

3. "PLEASURES" (Luke 8:14). In Mark 4:19 this thorn is listed as the "lusts for the remaining things," meaning those other than ordinary necessities of life. Sources of pleasure can act as thorns if our enjoyment of them becomes too extensive and too important. If we become addicted to them and are unhappy without them, they become thorns.

Pleasures often seem like necessities to us. I do not refer to the normal, average amount of recreation and pleasure which everyone should enjoy in order to live a balanced, healthy life. We should thank God for such enjoyable things (I Tim. 6:17). I rather refer to that tendency to become preoccupied with the pursuit of pleasure. Much self-control is necessary in this area. As interests shift in the direction of pleasures, there is less concern over the things of God. The answer is careful, intelligent restraint in the pursuit of recreation. Paul said not to use the things of this world in an unrestrained manner. (I Cor. 7:31).

4. RESULT OF CULTIVATION OF THORNS. There is a progression in this process described in Mark 4:19. A Christian worries about his daily needs—the necessities of life. Then he begins to think that money is the answer. The more money he earns, however, the more he spends and the more he wants. The result may be that his time, energy, and attention are monopolized by a preoccupation with worries, riches, and pleasures. A person involved in the pursuit of pleasure tends to neglect the things of God. He tends to lose interest in the Word of God, and the inevitable result is a lack of growth and decreased spirituality. This principle always holds true: A man must invest himself before he can expect fruit in return. Thorns must be uprooted before the spiritual life can prosper, and before God's will can be accomplished to the fullest.

The Lord Jesus in Luke 9:23 said that if any man "will come after me [be my disciple], let him deny himself . . . ." By "deny himself" the Lord means "let him be willing to give up his right to enjoy those luxuries and pleasures which would hinder his

Christian life." Christ's disciples had to give up many rights in order to serve the Lord (Matt. 19:27, 29). Today a man usually does not have to give up as much, depending upon the type of service to which the Lord directs him. But every Christian at times has to deny himself some things that would interfere with his Christian maturity and testimony. If the Christian is not willing to deny himself anything, for the sake of his Lord, then he cannot expect to bear much fruit. He must invest time, energy, and effort in order to reap spiritual profit.

Weights. The third cause of persistent immaturity is what the Bible calls "weights," or useless, unprofitable activities. I have put this problem in a different section because the Bible makes a distinction between "thorns" and "weights." "Weights" seem to be activities and things that are not sinful but which do not serve any spiritual purpose. They represent excess baggage which hinder spiritual progress and should be put aside (Heb. 12:1). Paul, in I Corinthians 6:12, says that all things are lawful but not all things are profitable. He goes on to point out that he will not be enslaved to these weights.

Thorns refer to things which tend to choke out the Word of God and stifle spiritual life. They are harmful and need to be uprooted whenever they are discovered. Weights are neither good nor bad, but may not be spiritually profitable. The use of them may not lead into sin, but they may consume valuable time and energy. So the question to be asked is not, "What's wrong with it?" but "Is it good for me?"

Hebrews 12:1 commands us to lay aside every weight so that we can run the race (our Christian career and life on earth) with patient endurance. If we try to run while burdened down with useless weights we will tire easily and fall short of endurance. No one receives a prize for carrying around a weight, but for running a race swiftly and efficiently. A good example of a weight is mentioned in II Timothy 2:3-4, where it says that a soldier who is going out to fight does not become entangled in civilian affairs, because this would make him less effective as a soldier. The lesson is that the Christian should not become too preoccupied with nonessential matters for fear of becoming less effective in his Christian walk.

In I Corinthians 9:26 Paul said he ran, but not uncertainly. By this he meant that he did not run in the wrong direction, wasting his time and energy. Paul said he fought, but not as beating the air. He did not direct his blows at nothing, but used his energy in efforts that were goal-directed.

It is necessary to maintain self-control. In I Corinthians 9:27, Paul said that he "keeps under" (literally, treats harshly) his body and "brings it into subjection" (literally, makes a slave out of it), lest he would end up disapproved by God. To "treat harshly" does not refer to senseless mistreatment of oneself, but rather to denying gratification of desires that would be spiritually harmful or would interfere with the Christian walk. The glutton is enslaved to food. If he had self-control he could deny himself food and stay on a reducing diet, thus losing his excess weight and becoming healthier. But a diet would be unpleasant and would cause some physical suffering. This is an example of what Paul meant when he said, "I treat my body harshly." This reminds us of the rigorous training and self-discipline of the olympic athlete. His self-control is for a worthwhile purpose.

We can discover the weights in our lives as we take stock of our spiritual progress. We may find ourselves slowed down by these weights, but as we cast them aside God causes us to become aware of other weights. As these weights drop off, it becomes easier for us to run the race.

Here is a specific example. A man is considering joining a monthly book club. If he reads these books as part of his normal recreation, this can be a good means of relaxation. On the other hand, if he already has sufficient recreation, the addition of such reading may crowd some spiritually useful activity out of his life. In such a case, the reading would be a weight.

The Effect of Spiritual Immaturity on Mental Health

THE PROBLEM

There are several consequences of spiritual immaturity. For

instance, addiction to material things produces vulnerability to depression. A lack of money can cause severe distress to a man who values it too highly. A housewife can let the task of doing her housework become too important and become depressed when she is temporarily unable to perform her household duties. The spiritually mature person does not allow unreliable things to become too important to him. However, life often involves great losses. The mature person can weather them, but the immature person is unprepared and may suffer a breakdown.

Furthermore, if a person is not growing spiritually into more maturity, then he may be drifting in his Christian life. This is dangerous because of the risk of becoming involved in and insensitive to sin (Heb. 3:13). If this happens it becomes necessary for God to chasten him, and this is never pleasant (I Cor. 11:32; 12:6, 11). And sin itself, apart from God's chastening, brings unpleasant mental consequences such as guilt and lowered feelings of self-esteem.

Moreover, the spiritually immature Christian usually lacks the knowledge of the Word and the wisdom to cope with the attack of Satan with his fiery darts (Eph. 6:16). Such a Christian is frequently swayed, misled, and upset by incorrect information (Eph. 4:13-14). Some people suffer great emotional anguish as they try in vain to live a sinlessly perfect life, thinking (incorrectly) that this is necessary to remain a Christian. In addition, the immature Christian tends to fail in utilizing all the help that is available from God. God gives grace to help those who come to Him (I Cor. 15:10; II Cor. 12:9; Heb. 4:16; James 4:6; I Peter 5:5). It is most supportive emotionally to be able to go to God in prayer about a distressing problem and have the assurance that He understands and will offer help (I Peter 5:7, 10).

THE REMEDY

The only real remedy is to maintain spiritual growth. This requires determination and careful avoidance or riddance of thorns and weights. Sometimes God must chasten us before we become willing to give up sin that hinders spiritual growth. But the necessary plan of action for growing in maturity is continued study of and meditation on the Word of God.

CHAPTER ELEVEN

ASSESSMENT OF PSYCHOLOGICAL AND SPIRITUAL MATURITY

FIRST OF ALL I shall try to explain briefly what I consider mature attitudes and behavior from both the psychological and spiritual viewpoint in several different areas.

Dependency

This term refers to the need each person has for emotional support, reassurance, guidance, or someone to lean on. If a person's dependency needs are abnormally great, then he is overly dependent and may ask and expect too much help from others. He may demand too much attention from others and thus aggravate them. This type of person is usually unable to make decisions for himself and tries to get others to make his decisions for him. He often seems insecure and repeatedly seeks reassurance about the same worry. A woman who is overly dependent is known as the helpless, clinging vine type. Such people find it hard to stand on their own two feet.

On the other hand, the person who represses his dependency needs becomes too independent. He does not permit himself to feel his need of others and may seem aloof and unfriendly. Or he may appear friendly, but never permit anything but superficial friendships to develop. Although he often helps others, he may find it hard to let others help him. Such a person does not want to depend on others, perhaps because he has been frustrated and hurt in the past when he reached out to someone for help.

There are good and bad ways of seeking dependency satis
faction. A healthy way is to turn to one's close family members
to a good friend, or to a pastor or doctor and ask for their advic
and support. Unhealthy ways would be to deliberately throw
nervous fit, to produce a crying spell, or to pretend to be sic
just to get attention and sympathy. Such devices are childish an
immature and are irritating to other people.

The Bible teaches that we are to help each other generousl
(Gal. 6:2; I Tim. 6:18; I Peter 4:8-9; I John 3:16-18). Yet at th
same time God wants us to use wisdom in trying to help other
(Col. 1:9). We should not rush in and do everything a fellov
Christian might want us to do, because the Bible also teaches u
to be healthily independent. For example, every man who is phys
ically able to work should earn his own living and not be finan
cially dependent on others (II Thess. 3:10-12). If a person re
ceives too much help he may become weak. Of course, a person
in deep mental or physical distress needs support, but when the
crisis is over he should be encouraged to help himself.

In summary, the mature person is able to be independent, ye
is also able to recognize his need for others. In times of need he
is able to reach out to others for help in a healthy and socially
acceptable way.

Hostility

The mature person recognizes that anger is a normal emotion
It is impossible to live in the world without occasionally being
provoked to anger by someone's offensive behavior. Any person
who is mistreated or who witnesses the cruel mistreatment of
others should experience some anger. We are commanded to be
angry at that which is wrong (Eph. 4:26). The emotion of anger
is not wrong in itself. Anger may be either reasonable or unreasonable. If a person becomes angry when there has been no
violation of his or another's personal rights as an individual, then
this is unreasonable anger. Moreover, there are good and bad
ways of expressing anger. The bad ways include such things as
name-calling, slander, cursing, physical attack (except in cases
of self-defense), and murder. Such expressions are condemned

by the Bible (Matt. 5:21-22; Eph. 4:31). Acceptable ways include such things as talking it over with a friend ("getting it off your chest") or talking it out with the person who has committed the offense. A person provoked to righteous anger has the right to express the anger in a verbal manner directly to the offender. This is not inconsistent with I Corinthians 13:5 which reads: "Love does not behave in an unseemly manner. It does not seek its own. It does not become irritated. It does not keep a record of the evil" (literal, expanded translation). This verse says that sometimes a Christian, out of love, when it seems to be the right thing to do for the sake of Christ, may give up his right to assert his anger and refrain from expressing it directly to the offender. It does not teach that he should *never* demand his rights nor express his anger. At times the only proper thing to do is to assert himself and demand his rights. For example, when he is being attacked physically it is certainly necessary for him to defend himself with a counterattack. God never intended Christians to permit others to walk all over them. Instead, God wants us to be men, yet men who can be self-controlled and gentle when the occasion warrants it.

In summary, the mature person becomes consciously angry whenever he is justified in doing so, yet expresses his anger when it is wise. When he does express his anger it is in an appropriate and acceptable way.

Aggression

Aggression refers to seeking and getting a desired object whether it is right or wrong. The mature person is normally aggressive. He is neither ruthless nor does he give up too easily in seeking his goals. He is persistent in working toward what he wants, yet he also uses wisdom and self-control. He does not believe that the end always justifies the means. The mature person also avoids wasting his energy in behavior that is not goal-directed. He does not scatter his efforts ineffectively, but tries to make them count in achieving his goals (I Cor. 9:26).

God wants us to be aggressive, especially about spiritual matters. He wants us to be zealous for that which is right and to run the race as if we are trying to win the prize (I Cor. 9:24; Heb. 12:1). Peter was a very aggressive man, and this characteristic made him useful in God's service.

In summary, aggression is determination and persistence in pressing toward a goal. Our goals should, of course, be consistent with our Christian standards.

Sex

The biological sexual drive is healthy and normal. The Bible never calls sex wrong. It is the use of sex that may be right or wrong. The Bible makes clear that God considers the uninhibited enjoyment of sexual relations inside marriage as free of any sin (I Cor. 7:3-5; Heb. 13:4). The mature adult finds his sexual drive directed toward a person of the opposite sex. The blocking (by some psychological problem) of this normal heterosexual drive may result in some sort of substitute or deviate sexual behavior, such as homosexuality or some other sexual perversion. Persistent masturbation in an adult who has a sexually normal marital partner available as a sexual object is also evidence of some inhibition of the normal sexual drive. Perhaps some psychological problem prevents the person from freely enjoying sexual relations with his mate. Any such blocking is labeled immaturity in the sense that the person has not reached the normal level in this area. The mature person recognizes his own sexual needs, chooses an appropriate marital partner and freely enjoys sexual relations without inhibitions or guilt within the limits of marriage.

Moreover, the mature person does desire sex with a normal frequency. The average varies anywhere from once per day to once every one or two weeks. The ability of a mature adult to have no need for sexual satisfaction and thus have no need for marriage requires a special gift of grace from God (I Cor. 7:7). Most Christians do not have such a gift. To remain single has only one advantage, that of permitting a person to serve the Lord free from the usual distractions of marriage and family life (I Cor. 7:33-34). This does not mean that the duties and pleasures of married life are in any way wrong or inferior. Marriage is honorable and wholesome. (Heb. 13:4).

And unless one has this special gift mentioned above, he will probably need sexual satisfaction, which God has made provision for in the institution of marriage (I Cor. 7:2, 9).

What about the person who does not have this special gift of not needing sex, who is not a homosexual and yet does not get married? The answer is that he either burns with sexual desire (I Cor. 7:9); or he engages in illicit sexual activities; or he sublimates his sexual desires into nonsexual activities which serve as a substitute outlet for his sexual energy. By sublimation he is able to maintain a psychological balance of a sort, although it tends to have a stifling effect on his personality, making him a less spontaneous person. Frequently there is a psychological problem which makes the person fear marriage. Sometimes external events (such as hardships of war) act to prevent marriage by removing marriage prospects.

Work

God has decreed that man must earn his living by working (Gen. 3:19; II Thess. 3:10-12). Thus we find in the psychological realm that a healthy, mature person will want to work. For a person to be deprived of any opportunity to work at some worthwhile activity is psychologically disturbing. The acceptance of the responsibility to work, the desire to do so, the consistent performance of the assigned tasks, and the enjoyment of work are all signs of maturity. Working requires the toleration of some delay in the gratification of his longings and the frustrations that result. Play has to come after the work is finished. The ability to tolerate a normal degree of frustration is a sign of maturity.

The extremes are signs of immaturity. At one extreme we have the irresponsible person who either refuses to work, or repeatedly manages to get fired from his job, or gets sick so he cannot work. It is usually too simple to say he is lazy, as this describes only the outward appearance. Inwardly such a person may be disturbed and in conflict. To want the privileges and benefits of life without accepting the accompanying responsibilities is unrealistic and leads to frustration and disappointment.

At the other extreme is the person who compulsively overworks.

This is not normal because it leads to fatigue and frustration of other normal needs. A person may overwork for various psychological reasons. Sometimes the purpose is to maintain a feeling of security. An insecure person may fear losing his job unless he double-checks his work and works extra hours. A person who thinks that wealth will bring security may get trapped in an endless chase after more and more money. Sometimes a person overworks so he can avoid thinking about unpleasant thoughts or disturbing problems. Work for him is a way of escape. Regardless of the reason, compulsive overworking is not normal. It is disrupting to the person's life, affecting his health, marriage, and family.

The need for and enjoyment of work is normal. This can become a problem in old age, since often a retired person becomes depressed after losing his work outlet. People expecting retirement should prepare for this need by seeking some useful activity or hobby or perhaps a part-time job.

Play

Christ recognized the normal human need to rest from working and enjoy the diversion of relaxing activities (Mark 6:31). This is a normal psychological need. For this reason God has provided us with a wide variety of activities for enjoyment (I Tim. 6:17). For instance, music is one of many things God has created for our relaxation. Everyone needs to develop and maintain some recreational outlets, and the mature person will do this without any feeling of guilt. Again a balance is necessary. Too much play leads to irresponsibility. And too much work is unhealthy also.

Relationships with Parents and Siblings

The mature adult should have a relationship with his parents, brothers, and sisters that is voluntary (that is, one that he genuinely wants) and is mutually satisfying. It should be governed by the same principles (such as mutual courtesy, politeness, friendliness, and respect for each other's rights and opinions) that would govern a friendly relationship with an outsider. The fact that parents have raised a child does not give them the right to demand special attention and services from their grown child or to violate his individual rights by trying to force their will upon him.

Parents are obligated to raise a child so that he can become financially and psychologically independent, not needing his parents anymore, able to stand on his own two feet. After this process is finished (presumably around age twenty-one) the grown child should not feel that he owes his parents anything. The one exception to this is to show them honor, which is defined and illustrated in the Bible as an obligation to help his parents in case of some desperate need, such as extreme poverty. (See Matt. 15:4-6; also I Tim. 5:4.) To honor one's parents does not mean that a grown child is obligated to cater to their every wish or pamper them. Nor does it mean that he is responsible for making a life for his parents or providing for their happiness. The parents should make a life for themselves and develop a set of friends and activities of their own. Their grown child (who usually has a family, friends, and interests of his own) should only be active in their life as he chooses since this is a privilege, not an obligation.

It is wrong for parents to think of raising children for the purpose of using them for their own selfish needs such as financial support. To the contrary, the Bible states that the parents are responsible for making some attempt to accumulate an estate and to leave an inheritance to their children (II Cor. 12:14). The mature person will feel free to make a life for himself based upon his own needs and the needs of his family, even though this might conflict with what his elderly parents want.

Relationship with a Marital Partner

Ordinarily the mature person gets married by the time he is around thirty years old (at least the early thirties; no exact figure can be given). When a person is past thirty and still not married, then there is a chance that some psychological problem has made him avoid marriage. There are, of course, exceptions to this principle, such as a doctor who tries to finish a long course of training and education before marriage. Still, in such circumstances the need to marry frequently asserts itself and he finds himself wanting to marry even before he finishes his training. Financial considerations would, of course, affect his decision to marry or wait. Many men have married while still in training and their wives have worked until their husbands finished their education and found regular jobs. Sometimes a person may mature more slowly than the average, not becoming ready for marriage until after he has reached his thirties.

I need to make it clear that the person who has a psychological problem that makes him fear marriage is not necessarily a bad mental case. To the contrary, many such people are skilled in some occupation and occupy a useful place in society. There are also some people who are so involved in their work or profession that they should not try to be married. Marriage, like anything else, requires an investment of time, energy, and interest to make it work. For example, the hardworking businessman who works seventy to eighty hours a week on the job perhaps should not be married and also work such hours.

Moreover, the mature person has good reasons for getting married to a certain person at a certain time. For example, a young fifteen-year-old girl who marries just to get away from an unhappy home makes a mistake. This is not a sound basis for starting a marriage. Some people, fearing domination by others, will marry weak or nonassertive partners. They reason that in this way they can avoid being controlled by their partner. A weak marital partner may not be dominating, but he may not be capable or responsible either, and may neglect his marital duties. Some people marry trying to replace a lost parent or to gain a parent they never had in childhood. This usually produces some marital dissatisfaction, since a marital partner cannot also be a parent. A parent-child relationship is one-sided in that the parent does most of the giving and the child does most of the taking. Such a one-sided relationship is not normal in an adult marital relationship, where the giving and the taking (that is, the enjoyment of the benefits of marriage) should be about equal for each partner.

The mature person will have sound reasons for marrying. He

will love his wife; he will pick her because she comes close to the physical, psychological, social, moral and spiritual ideal he is looking for; she will have the type of personality he wants; and she will share the same general ambitions and goals that he has. After marriage the mature person will continue to love his partner, forming a close, solid bond. He will be able to communicate to his partner many of his deeper thoughts (not necessarily all of them) and will urge his partner to do the same. He will desire and permit a satisfying intimacy or closeness. He will desire and enjoy free and uninhibited sexual relations with his mate, being careful to be equally concerned about giving her satisfaction also. He will form the habit of turning to his wife for satisfaction of his needs and avoid situations where another woman could become too important to him. The concept of a close, intimate love in marriage is taught by the Bible (Eph. 5:25, 28, 33).

The principle of authority is also clear. The mature husband freely discusses things with his wife and wants her to share in family decisions. But he is willing to take the responsibility for making the final decision whenever there is uncertainty or a lack of agreement between the two. The mature wife will assert herself and freely express her opinions and wishes, but she will accept her husband's final decision. Thus the normal pattern is for the wife to be slightly more dependent upon the husband (Eph. 5:22-24; I Tim. 3:4-5; Titus 2:5; I Peter 3:1, 5). The mature husband, in making his decisions, decides on the basis of what is best for the family as a whole, not on the basis of what he particularly wants as an individual.

Relationships with Peers

By peers I mean people of the same approximate age, social status, and circumstances—in other words, friends and acquaintances, business and personal. The mature person will tend to reach out to his peers with friendly overtures, but he will be discriminating. He would not seek the friendship of someone he disliked, motivated by a fear of disapproval. Nor would he permit his friends to dominate him or try to dominate them. Instead, he would try to achieve a balance of equal give and take. The need for reaching out to others is important. Some people have few friends simply because they do not reach out often enough with friendliness (Prov. 18:24). The mature person does not avoid people, nor is he too dependent upon friends. The healthy attitude is to need others, but not as a crutch. Another evidence of immaturity is to have too strong a tendency to compete with others. It is normal to want to win, but not to become sick over losing. The mature person enjoys and is enjoyed by his friends. He also holds his own with his business associates, neither dominating nor being dominated by them.

Relationship with Self

The mature person has a realistic self-image. He neither underestimates nor overestimates himself. His self-image is close to what he really is. For example, if a man is good at intellectual pursuits but poor at athletics, then it is unrealistic for him to think of himself as an excellent athlete. He does not have an inferiority complex, nor does he tend to tell himself how much better he is than others. It is immature and unspiritual to always be comparing ourselves with others (II Cor. 10:12). The mature person has sufficient self-confidence so that he does not feel threatened and become anxious or hostile when someone else disagrees with him or excels in some way over him. He does not have an overly severe conscience so that he berates himself for his failures. Instead he tries to learn from his mistakes and thus improve his performance and behavior.

The mature person acts his age. There should be only one childhood, not two, and it should end somewhere around the age of twenty-one. And an adult should not spend too much time living in his inward world—daydreaming and unresponsive to the external world. To prefer to daydream about life rather than actually live it is abnormal and thus a sign of immaturity. However, a certain amount of daydreaming is normal in everyone.

In summary, the mature person perceives himself realistically, does not consider himself inferior or worthless, and does not spend too much time living in fantasy.

Relationship with Outer World of Reality

The mature person will accept reality even if the truth is unpleasant and disturbing to him. He will tend to face up to the truth rather than flee from it. He will perceive the situation as it really is and make a rational, logical, and intelligent decision as to how to cope with it. Sometimes a situation is so hopeless or dangerous that the proper solution is to flee from it. But here the flight occurs as a result of facing the problem and deciding upon a solution. The immature person may seek some means of escape instead of facing the problem and trying to cope with it. It is a well-known fact that alcoholics use alcohol as an escape mechanism to flee from their problems. Others develop behavior patterns which are actually methods of avoiding problems. For example, a shy student may consistently arrive in class a few minutes late in order to avoid having to talk to other students.

The mature person tends to keep reevaluating his experiences and his perceptions of the world and life. He does not become rigid and fixed in his opinions so that when new truth is presented to him he is unable to change his mind. Such a person is considered dogmatic and rigid by others. We ought to keep on learning throughout our lives, especially from our mistakes. The tendency to be unwilling to admit an error of judgment or mistake in behavior in the past and to refuse to correct an erroneous opinion is evidence of immaturity. The Christian is told that God will reveal to him his incorrect and immature attitudes (Phil. 3:15). The rigid person who will not change his mind, even when the facts indicate the need for a change in attitude, is frequently an insecure person who actually is unsure of his own conviction. There is nothing disgraceful about being unsure about an issue when lacking in sufficient information to make an intelligent decision. Yet the insecure person seems to feel he must decide anyway, whether right or wrong, and must forever stick to his decision. The mature person wants to know if he is wrong about something and wants to correct his error as soon as possible.

A similar type of immaturity is seen in the inflexible person.

He has a tendency to want to do things in exactly the same way he has always done them in the past, even though circumstances have created a definite need for a change in procedure. Again here we sense the feeling of insecurity in such a person. He feels anxious about trying anything new or different even though there may be sound reasons for a change. Life is full of changing situations, and the mature person is flexible enough to adapt himself to a new situation by a change of procedure without feeling that he has to compromise on a moral or ethical principle. He will also recognize and accept the principle that responsibility and priviliges go together. This rule applies whether it is a new car one is buying or a girl one is courting. A mature person will not try to buy a car unless he is able to pay for it in a responsible way. When he does buy it he will conscientiously make his payments on time. Likewise, a mature person will not expect to gain the friendship and love of a girl he is courting without being friendly to her and offering love to her also. Similarly, the mature person accepts the fact that he has to work if he expects to keep his job and receive wages.

To summarize, the mature person perceives the outward world as it really is and adapts himself to it as well as possible, without compromising his moral convictions and sacrificing his own character.

Freedom from Persistent Mental Symptoms

Everyone has had some unhappy experiences in childhood as well as disappointments in adult life. Some resultant symptoms or behavior patterns, such as persistent anxiety and depression, often hinder him from living a normal life. An example is a phobia, or abnormal fear, which prevents normal geographical movement in everyday life. It is impossible to live in the world today and experience upsets, insults, attacks, and other disappointments without sometimes responding with some depression or anxiety. But the mature person does not persist in these symptoms too long. A good illustration is the mourning process after the loss of a loved one. The mature person is normally depressed after such an experience. But his depression is neither incapacitating nor permanent. He eventually gets over his depression and is back to his usual self. He has adjusted to the changed life situation. However, the immature person may be unable to function at all, and may never make a satisfactory adjustment to his changed life situation.

In summary, the mature person is usually free from mental symptoms which interfere in his life and prevent a normal functioning and adjustment.

Relationship to God

Some people tend to relate to God as if He were another parent. So if a Christian's relationship to his parents in childhood was relatively normal, then his relationship to God will probably be free of peculiar and distorted attitudes. However, the immature person may tend to think of God in a distorted and inaccurate way. For example, a person who had to battle a tyranical father in childhood may tend to think of God as a tyrant also. This arouses rebellion and makes it harder for such a person to yield himself to God. Thus it may hinder him from forming a good spiritual relationship with God.

The mature person is independent enough so that he is psychologically free to make a decision to commit his life to God if he wants to do so. He also has sufficient self-control so that he can make his decision of yieldedness to God effective in his life from day to day. He thus has the ability to say no to himself and yes to God, whenever the occasion warrants it. The immature person may lack this sort of self-control. It is true that in every human being there is a certain amount of reluctance to obey God and a tendency to want one's own way. In the Bible this tendency is called the "flesh" or "sin nature" or "old man." The mature person, after he has become a Christian, is able to utilize the help available from God so that he can manifest obedience to God in spite of the tendency to disobey. This is in contrast to the immature person whose mind may be so preoccupied with psychological problems that he is not mentally free to give sufficient thought to obeying God.

Ability to Apply Spiritual Truth

It is granted that we cannot manifest this ability without God's help (I Cor. 2:9-16; Gal. 5:16-18). But it is a complicated process involving several different steps. At different points in the process we may be hindered not only by a lack of spiritual knowledge or devotion to God, but also by a lack of maturity. First, a lack of maturity may make it hard for the Christian to make the definite decision to yield his life to God. Then, if he does yield himself to God, immaturity may make it hard for him to carry out day-by-day obedience and remain devoted to God. His immaturity may then give rise to numerous prejudices which may make it hard for him to be objective in studying and understanding spiritual truth. Immaturity may also prevent him from making the proper and appropriate application of the truth. He may either try to apply it where it does not fit, or he may not see the proper situation where it should apply.

Moreover, once having made the application and seeing how he should behave, the immature person may lack sufficient self-control to behave in the proper way, even with God's available help. Self-control is a fruit of God the Holy Spirit (see Gal. 5:23). But the Spirit has to work through the person's mind, which may or may not be functioning efficiently. Self-control is the end result of the Holy Spirit working through a mind that is functioning normally. There are many people who are not even Christians that have quite a bit of self-control because they have a mind that is functioning normally. Immaturity often prevents the Christian from receiving the full benefit of God's available help.

Interaction of Physical, Psychological and Spiritual Factors

There are several different sets of relationships here. Physical disorders lower one's resistance to psychological disorders because it is hard to be emotionally stable when the body is weak or sick. Of course some mental conditions are caused directly by physical disease, as has been discussed earlier in this book. It is also true that a psychological disorder may lower one's resistance to physical disease. For instance, a man under great nervous tension may develop a stomach ulcer. Likewise an emotional upset, perhaps unrelated to the disease, can aggravate a person's condition when he has a physical illness.

Now a person's ability to utilize spiritual truth and appropriate spiritual help from God may be decreased by either physical or psychological distress or disease. Thus we should not be surprised at spiritual failures during such times. Moreover, spiritual failures in turn tend to discourage and depress the Christian and this tends to aggravate his psychological and/or physical distress.

The recognition of each independent factor causing a person to be nervous sometimes is simple but at other times it is quite complicated. I recommend that such a person first have a complete physical checkup from his family doctor, including a general physical examination, a neurological examination, proper laboratory studies (such as blood tests, etc.), and X-rays of any area of suspected disease, including chest and skull X-rays. Factors such as overwork, lack of sufficient recreation, menopausal age, and similar conditions should alert the doctor to the presence of possible fatigue or the effect of a physiological process. If the person is physically fit, then the psychological and spiritual factors should be investigated. The approach here can be oriented along the lines of the known needs of that person. These needs have been discussed previously in chapter 7. Any needs which seem abnormal, either in strength or in character, should be taken into account. Notice whether the person's life provides adequate satisfaction for the basic, normal needs. To neglect a need or to reject a need as unworthy and fail to satisfy it may lead to psychological tension and distress. Also the seeming absence of a need is significant. For example, if a person has no friends at all and seems to need no friends, it probably means that his awareness of the need is choked off. It has been repressed into the subconscious mind, where it continues to exert a pull, acting as a source of unhappiness.

In effect we need to think in terms of three different sets of causative factors: physical, psychological, and spiritual. The physical can be evaluated accurately only by a medical doctor. To evaluate the spiritual, one does not have to be a pastor, but he does have to know and understand spiritual truth and its proper application to everyday life situations. To evaluate the psychological in a thorough way requires the consultation of a psychiatrist or psychologist. However, many nonpsychiatric personnel, such as pastors and counselors can be helpful. In fact the patients themselves can learn enough about psychological principles so that they can recognize them when these factors are present. It helps the counselor to have a history of the patient's symptoms and behavior provided by others (such as family or friends) who know the patient. They can frequently add important information which makes the picture more clear. Serious disappointments and drastic changes in the person's life situation (such as deaths in the family, loss of a job, etc.) tend to upset his emotional balance and require readjustment.

The presence of nervous symptoms in a Christian is not necessarily associated with sin or spiritual failure. If there is sin it should be acknowledged and confessed (I John 1:9). But it is also important to discover any undesirable habits or tendencies (perhaps related to underlying psychological problems) which lie behind the spiritual failure. Poor spiritual habits as well as unhealthy psychological and physical habits should be recognized and corrected so as to possibly prevent future repetition of the sin. If the person claims he has no unconfessed sin then the counselor should tentatively accept this and not be like Job's friends who unjustly accused Job of sin (Job 32:3). Even after sin has been confessed, there may be some unpleasant consequences that have to be faced. Although God has forgiven him, the Christian still may have to reap what he has sown. For example, the businessman who is caught cheating on his income tax has committed a crime as well as a sin. God will forgive him when he confesses his sin, but he still will have to pay a penalty such as a fine or a prison term.

If a Christian has no qualified counselor to help him he should ask God's help in evaluating and analyzing himself (I Cor. 11:31-32; II Cor. 13:5).

Identification of Psychological Disorders

In this section I will give a brief outline of the symptoms of psychological distress.

Notice the Thoughts

1. Are there illogical or bizarre thoughts?
2. Are there delusions (especially of being controlled, persecuted, etc.) or hallucinations (hearing voices, seeing visions, etc.)?
3. Is there serious denial of reality (such as, claiming a dead relative to be still living)?
4. Are his thoughts (as he talks along) interrupted by strange and abrupt silences (called "blocking")?
5. Are his thoughts organized so that he is able to make his point? Or does he ramble aimlessly from one subject to another?
6. Are his religious convictions absurd by ordinary logical and/or scriptural standards?
7. Does he have a normal conscience? Is it too strict, or not strict enough?
8. Is his judgment intact?
9. Are his intellectual powers functioning properly? (Can he add and subtract? Does he know where he is? Does he know the date?)

Notice the Mood

1. Is he anxious?
2. Is he fearful? Are the fears related to illogical or trivial things?
3. Is he depressed?
4. Is he contemplating suicide?

Notice the Affect (Emotions)

1. Does he seem devoid of any emotion? Flat? Blank?
2. Is the emotion he does show appropriate in quantity and/or character to the experience which he is having or describing? For example, does he laugh when he should cry?

3. Does he experience hostile feelings that are inappropriate and unreasonable?
4. Does he experience sexual feelings that are inappropriate and/or deviate?
5. Does he experience religious feelings that are inappropriate and/or inconsistent with reality or logic?

NOTICE THE BEHAVIOR

1. Does he exhibit hostile behavior that is unreasonable, uncontrollable, or socially or morally unacceptable?
2. Does he exhibit sexual behavior that is deviate, uncontrollable, or socially or morally unacceptable?
3. Does he exhibit religious behavior that is bizarre or that is based upon illogical convictions?
4. Does he exhibit behavior patterns that are useless (such as repeated handwashing), or self-destructive (such as suicidal attempt), or harmful to others (such as compulsive lying or stealing)?
5. Does he exhibit a tendency to withdraw from people and from life?
6. Does he exhibit a tendency to regress to childish behavior patterns?
7. Does he exhibit a behavior problem, which he calls a "spiritual problem," but which does not respond to any of the usual spiritual remedies?

Spiritual Remedies

Here we must define our terms. A *disorder* is a group of one or more psychological problems producing symptoms which combine to cause mental suffering or to interfere with the person's ability to function effectively. Disorders are usually labeled on the basis of the type of symptom which predominates. A *problem* is the specific fear, mistaken idea, or abnormal longing which lies at the root of the disorder and which gives rise to the symptoms. Now the question is: Can spiritual remedies ever be useful in helping psychological problems? The answer is, yes, sometimes. They may be useful in several ways. First, they can offer temporary relief of some of the distressing symptoms. But this is comparable to taking an aspirin for fever. It fails to get at the cause of the symptoms, and they usually return sooner or later unless the problem is resolved. Second, spiritual remedies can be used to help the person face up to the psychological problem that needs to be resolved. For example, the exhortation from and prayer with another Christian may help put pressure on a person to admit to himself what his problem really is. Thus he may be encouraged to face it and try to solve it. The basic psychological problem, whatever it is, still is cleared up only when it is faced up to and the appropriate psychological remedy is applied.

Listed below are some spiritual helps with related Bible verses.

Spiritual Remedies or Helps

1. Maintain the vessel (the person) in good physical and psychological condition (Mark 6:31).
2. Be submissive to God rather than rebellious (James 4:6-7; I Peter 5:5-6).
3. Make the decision to yield your life to God and to carry out His will for your life (Ps. 37:5; Rom. 6:13; 12:1).
4. Having yielded yourself to God, try daily to be obedient to Him (I Sam. 15:22-23; I Peter 3:10-11).
5. Confess to God any known sin (I John 1:9).
6. Try to put to use any truth you learn ("Walk in the light," I John 1:7).
7. Try to profit from the discipline of testing (Rom. 5:3-5; 8:28; II Cor. 12:7-10; Heb. 5:8; 12:5-11; James 1:3-4).
8. Set the goal of becoming spiritually educated through Bible study (Eph. 4:13-14; Col. 1:9-10; I Peter 2:2).
9. Permit yourself to be exhorted or rebuked by other Christians when needed (Gal. 6:1; I Tim. 5:20; Titus 1:13; Heb. 10:25).
10. Acquire the habit of intelligent and bold prayer (Eph. 6:18; I Thess. 5:17; Heb. 4:16; James 1:5).
11. Fight the fight of faith (Prov. 3:5; Eph. 6:16; James 1:6; I Peter 4:19; 5:7).

12. Be willing to wait upon God (Ps. 27:14; 37:7; I Peter 5:10).
13. Understand that the Holy Spirit will help with His power as you consciously try to achieve your goal (Col. 1:11, 29).

Misuse of Spiritual Remedies

The most common misuse is that of stubbornly insisting upon the use of a spiritual remedy, such as faith or prayer, when there is clear evidence of a psychological problem. The problem continues to manifest itself in spite of all efforts to apply spiritual remedies. In my experience this sort of situation often represents an attempt to avoid facing the problem. The truth is sometimes very painful to face, but God wants the Christian to recognize the truth so that he can make a proper adjustment to it. God wants us to walk in the light, not in darkness (I John 1:7). Some Christians want to get around the problem without solving it. They ask God to make the symptoms go away instead of asking Him to help them discover the cause of the symptoms—that is, the problem. Such a Christian is more interested in being comfortable and free from symptoms than in maturing. God wants us to be comfortable, but He also wants us to be mature, useful vessels for His service. But maturation involves awareness of psychological problems and sound, healthy adjustment to them, God wants us to have an accurate self-image (Rom. 12:3; Gal. 6:3), and to evaluate and judge ourselves (I Cor. 11:31-32).

Need for Breakdown in Some Cases

I have presented earlier the concept of hiding from a problem by pushing it into the subconscious mind and erecting defenses to avoid recognition of it. A problem thus buried cannot be resolved since the person is not conscious of it. One type of nervous breakdown represents a transfer of such a problem into the conscious mind, accompanied by feelings of anxiety, fear, and depression. This occurs so rapidly that the mind is overwhelmed by the excess of emotions and cannot continue to function effectively. This produces a breakdown. Although the person may be temporarily disabled psychologically, his problem is no longer hidden. Once the problem is out in the open he can be persuaded to cope with it instead of hiding from it. So sometimes a breakdown can lead to improvement. But this is doing it the hard way. Psychotherapy aims at letting the problem emerge from the subconscious in a slow, gradual, and safe manner so that the problem can be faced without arousing too much anxiety which might precipitate a breakdown. A person who does suffer a breakdown can then expect improvement if he faces up to his problem and makes the necessary adjustment to it. God can repair the damage (I Peter 5:10).

Psychological Invalids?

Sometimes a person can suffer so much physical damage during his developmental years that in adulthood his body cannot be changed or corrected. (A good example is a fracture of a leg bone which may leave one leg shorter than the other or deformed in some way.) The same principle is true in the psychological realm. A person can suffer so much abuse and mistreatment and be so damaged psychologically during the developmental years that it is impossible for him to ever resolve all the resulting psychological problems. The damage may be so great that he will be unable to function successfully in society as an adult. No amount of psychiatric treatment will ever make him normal. Of course God could heal such a person miraculously if He chose to do so. But God does not usually do this, since it would be acting contrary to His natural laws. What can be done for such a person? Psychiatrists can provide such things as tranquilizers which can give some relief from the psychological suffering and also can help the person function more effectively in society. Treatment in a mental hospital may help some. Simple encouragement (supportive psychotherapy) helps others. Other Christians can encourage such persons to keep going, as well as to be tolerant of them (Gal. 6:2). Paul said to be patient toward all and to give support to the weak and encourage the fainthearted (I Thess. 5:14). Moreover, sometimes these psychological invalids will develop strong inner motivation and will begin trying (where they have not tried before) and will surprise everyone by their improvement.

I wish to stress the fact that most people with nervous problems are not psychological invalids. It is a rare case for a Christian to be a psychological cripple with no real chance of improvement; but it does happen. God has promised us grace to help in time of need (Heb. 4:16). Notice it says grace to help, not grace to cure. God has promised never to leave or forsake you, and He will help you to endure the problem (Heb. 13:5). Even though the Christian is suffering, God is still with him, and even though he often cannot feel God's presence, he can know, by faith, that God is with him.

CHAPTER TWELVE

SUMMARY—RULES FOR GOOD MENTAL HEALTH

ALTHOUGH THERE IS some overlapping here with the list of spiritual remedies outlined in chapter 11, I have tried to formulate a set of rules based on the principles discussed in this book. These are rules which, if followed, would eliminate much mental turmoil and unrest of soul among Christians. I do not claim that all mental unrest would be eliminated, because trials, sorrows, and heartbreaks will always occur and will affect us. But some measure of peace can be regained if one follows the right procedure. We should try to make these rules habits, as a man is made or broken by his habits.

Suggested Rules or Habits for Good Mental Health

1. Live a carefully balanced life, paying attention to God's rules governing the body and mind in regard to the proper amount of rest and relaxation along with work.
2. Maintain your physical health as well as possible. This in turn will help you maintain good mental health.
3. Develop those mental attitudes which will permit you to give adequate, proper outward expression to your strong emotions.
4. Develop habits which include morally and socially acceptable ways of expressing these strong emotions. Do not keep emotions bottled up.
5. Aside from your regular work, develop and maintain some recreational outlets to help release tension.

6. Try to find someone you can trust and confide in. Everyone needs someone to talk to.

7. Go after what you want in life, aiming for the right kind of goals.

8. Take some appropriate action as soon as possible when your security is threatened in any realm.

9. Face up to reality. Do not run away from problems.

10. If a situation is really impossible to live with, flee from it. For example, a wife may have to leave a brutal, alcoholic husband who tries to kill her.

11. Develop a social life sufficient for your social needs. Do not be a recluse, withdrawn from people.

12. Recognize God's existence and get right with Him. Become a Christian.

13. Avoid doing that which is morally wrong, so as to avoid the feeling of guilt.

14. After becoming a Christian, yield your life to God (Rom. 12:1). Then try to maintain a close, personal relationship to Him.

15. Do not fight against God, obey Him (James 4:6-7).

16. Walk in the light; be obedient to God's laws, no matter what happens (I John 1:7).

17. Maintain a good conscience (I Tim. 1:19), and confess your sins to God (I John 1:9).

18. Walk in the energy of God the Holy Spirit instead of depending on the energy of the flesh (Gal. 5:16).

19. Walk by faith instead of by sight (II Cor. 5:7; I Tim. 1:19).

20. Be careful as to what you put first in importance in your life.

21. Aim toward Christian maturity. Feed regularly upon the Word of God and maintain regular communion through prayer with the Person of God.

22. Avoid thorns and weights that choke spiritual and psychological growth (Mark 4:19; Heb. 12:1).

23. Take a stand against Satan (Eph. 6:13; I Peter 5:8).

24. Cast every overly anxious worry into the lap of God and trust Him to either dispose of it or help you handle it

effectively (I Peter 5:7). If you do this the peace of God can guard your mind and heart against the unsettling and damaging effects of excess worry (Phil. 4:6-7).

25. Try to think about the right kind of things (Phil. 4:8).
26. Have the right attitude toward problems.

This includes: (1) Looking for your own faults, (2) accepting some problems as tests from God, designed to produce a good end result, (3) considering problems as opportunities for further improvement, (4) trying to avoid the tendency to murmur, (5) accepting some problems as a part of everyday life, (6) being willing to accept problems (if incurable) and ask God for grace to help tolerate the distress they cause.

The Apostle Paul makes a profound statement in I Timothy 6:6: "Godliness with contentment is great gain." The word contentment means "self-sufficiency." This does not mean that the sufficiency comes from oneself, but that it is found *within oneself.* This verse suggests that the man who finds satisfaction for the needs of his soul is a rich man. Paul in this verse links godliness with contentment because the two are closely related. Godliness means "having the right attitude toward and behaving properly toward God." A godly man is one who agrees with God and tries to pattern his behavior after God, living a life of obedience to God's commandments.

The author of Ecclesiastes, probably King Solomon, stated that he had tried everything that the world had to offer: wisdom, riches, pleasure, eating, and labor. Yet he did not find that which satisfied his soul. In Ecclesiastes 6:7 he points out that, although man may labor, yet "the appetite [literally, soul] is not filled." His conclusion was that everything in the world when not properly related to God is vanity (12:8). Then in Ecclesiastes 12:13, Solomon gives the conclusion he came to regarding the right way for man to find satisfaction. He says: "Let us hear the conclusion of the whole matter: Fear God, and keep his commandments: for this is the whole duty of man."

The creature cannot ignore the laws of his Creator; therefore men must submit themselves to God, manifesting this submission by obedience to His laws. The man who finds peace of mind is the one who submits himself to God and who obeys God's commandments (James 4:7). And the man who resists God will find that God in turn resists him (v. 6).

SUBJECT INDEX

SCRIPTURE INDEX

188